Cooking School

ITALIAN

Cooking School
ITALIAN

Bring the flavours of Italy to life in your own kitchen!

This edition published in 2011
LOVE FOOD is an imprint of Parragon Books Ltd

Parragon
Queen Street House
4 Queen Street
Bath BA1 1HE, UK

www.parragon.com

ISBN: 978-1-4454-7027-6

Printed in China

Internal design by Pink Creative

Notes for the Reader

This book uses both metric and imperial measurements. Follow the same units of measurement throughout; do not mix metric and imperial. All spoon measurements are level: teaspoons are assumed to be 5 ml, and tablespoons are assumed to be 15 ml. Unless otherwise stated, milk is assumed to be full fat, eggs and individual vegetables are medium, and pepper is freshly ground black pepper.

The times given are an approximate guide only. Preparation times differ according to the techniques used by different people and the cooking times may also vary from those given. Optional ingredients, variations or serving suggestions have not been included in the calculations.

Recipes using raw or very lightly cooked eggs should be avoided by infants, the elderly, pregnant women, convalescents and anyone suffering from an illness. Pregnant and breastfeeding women are advised to avoid eating peanuts and peanut products. Sufferers from nut allergies should be aware that some of the ready-made ingredients used in the recipes in this book may contain nuts. Always check the packaging before use.

Contents

Introduction

As a nation with one of the longest and most complex culinary histories, the Italians take their cuisine very seriously. It is an innate part of the culture and plays an important role in local traditions and history. Cooking and eating are synonymous with conviviality, good company and good wine, and for most Italians life revolves around mealtimes, whether at home or at one of the many types of restaurant.

Despite increasingly busy lifestyles, many Italians still make daily trips to the local market or delicatessen to buy the freshest and best produce available. Although ingredients are available year round, Italians have always preferred to eat locally grown foods at the time of year when they are fully ripe and the flavour is at its best – a concept other developed countries are only just beginning to take on board.

Regional Variations

Before Italy's unification in 1870, the country was made up of numerous small republics and kingdoms – each area a tightly knit community with its own particular cuisine. What was eaten depended on geographical region as well as culture.

In the fertile plains of the north, dairy products and beef were common. Even today, butter is used more than oil for cooking and many sauces are based on cream or cheese made from cow's milk. In the hot and arid south, the diet was more frugal, based on olive oil, vegetables, fish and cheeses made from sheep's or goat's milk. Coastal areas obviously made best use of seafood, while in mountainous regions cured meats that could be stored for long periods were an important part of the cuisine.

Rice was an important staple in Lombardy, the Po Valley and the Venetian hinterland. Along with polenta, it was considered the food of the poor and was often combined with simple ingredients as in Risotto Primavera. Baked polenta was another plain but sustaining dish that made the most of whatever ingredients were to hand. Nowadays, both rice and polenta continue to feature prominently on regional menus in restaurants ranging from the most basic *osteria* to the grandest *trattoria*.

Each region had, and still has, its own bread: big-holed chewy ciabatta in the north, dense unsalted white bread in Tuscany and gigantic crusty wheels of rough country bread in Puglia in the south.

Likewise, pasta has regional variations. In the north it is often freshly made with egg – perfect for absorbing creamy sauces. In the south the pasta is hard and dry, and made with durum wheat and water only. This type is more suitable for oil- or tomato-based sauces.

Although similar dishes are now found throughout the country, thanks to modern food-storage and transport systems, each of Italy's twenty regions remains fiercely proud of its individual culinary identity. True to form, Italians continue to be strongly attached to authentic food and long-held culinary traditions, while at the same time making the most of contemporary tastes and new ideas.

Essential Italian Ingredients

Most basic Italian ingredients can be stored for months. As you build up your supplies, you'll always have the makings of a delicious meal.

OLIVE OIL

Graded according to international standards; the lower the acidity, the better the flavour. Should be stored in a cool dark place; best bought in cans or dark bottles.

Extra virgin, first cold-pressed: the finest grade, superb peppery flavour and fruity aroma. Use for dressing salads and grilled vegetables, and bread-dipping.

Virgin: the next-best grade after extra virgin, reasonable flavour. Use for cooking rather than in dressings.

Olive oil, or pure olive oil: a blend of refined, virgin and extra virgin oils, bland flavour.

CHEESES

Fontina: smooth cow's milk cheese for melting into sauces and gratins. Sweet, buttery, mild flavour.

Gorgonzola: sharp, creamy blue cheese made from cow's milk. Excellent flavouring for pasta sauces and soups. Also served as a table cheese.

Mascarpone: cow's milk cream cheese with very high fat content (40–50%). Used for enriching pasta sauces, baked dishes and desserts.

Mozzarella: slightly stringy, milky-white cheese that melts well. The best is made from water buffalo's milk, but cow's milk mozzarella is more widely available. Use it fresh in salads, as a pizza topping, or baked in lasagne.

Parmigiano-Reggiano (Parmesan): hard cow's milk cheese made to a strict traditional formula. Complex nutty flavour with slightly crystalline texture. Used mainly for grating, though also served as a table cheese when moist and young. Grate just before using.

Pecorino Romano: hard sheep's milk cheese with crumbly texture and sharp flavour. Used as a grating cheese.

Ricotta: soft fresh unsalted cheese made with cow's milk whey. Mild flavour suitable for both savoury and sweet dishes. Use for stuffed pasta, dips, sauces, pastries and tarts.

MEATS – CURED

Pancetta: similar to streaky bacon. Sold cubed or in thin slices.

Parma ham: pale sweet-tasting ham. Must come from pigs weighing over 150 kg/330 lb and must be air-dried in specific regions of northern Italy.

Salami: comes in enormous variety of sizes and flavourings with regional specialities.

FISH AND SEAFOOD – CURED

Anchovies: brine-cured or salted fillets. Use in pizza, salads, dips and sauces, and for flavouring meat and vegetable dishes. Will deepen other flavours without imparting a fishy taste.

Clams: available in cans or jars. Add to pasta sauces or risotto.

Tuna: packed in oil or brine. Invaluable for salads and pasta sauces.

PASTA – DRIED

There are two basic types: pasta made with hard durum wheat flour (semolina) and water, and egg pasta made with plain flour and eggs. Pasta comes in an extraordinary number of shapes, each lending itself to a particular type of sauce. Long round pasta is best with tomato- or oil-based sauces that cling to the pasta; tubes and shapes are ideal for trapping chunkier sauces in their crevices. Egg pasta is more absorbent and best with butter- or cream-based sauces.

RISOTTO RICE

The short oval grains of risotto rice have a high starch content, which gives risotto its characteristic creaminess. Arborio is the best-known variety, but vialone nano and carnaroli are also both widely available.

POLENTA

A staple food in northern Italy, polenta is coarsely ground cornmeal. Depending on the amount of water added, polenta may be served wet, like mashed potato, or cooled and cut into shapes for grilling or frying.

PULSES

Beans, lentils and chickpeas are used throughout Italy but are particularly popular in Tuscany and Umbria. They are sold dried or in cans. Dried pulses need lengthy soaking and cooking but have a better flavour.

HERBS

Fresh herbs are best but, if necessary, rosemary, thyme, sage, marjoram and oregano may be used dried. Make sure you buy chopped dried leaves rather than ground powder. Use 1 teaspoon dried herbs in place of 1 tablespoon fresh herbs.

PINE KERNELS

Oily cream-coloured kernels with a slightly sweet flavour. An essential ingredient in pesto, and also used in biscuits and cakes.

Hints and Tips

Italian cooking is wonderfully straightforward but it is worth mastering a few tricks of the trade to increase your confidence.

Making Fresh Pasta Dough

- Unlike pastry, pasta responds well to warmth. Never work on a marble board; instead use a large wooden board or other smooth, relatively warm material.
- For the best results use Italian '00' flour.
- Rolling by hand: knead the dough for at least 10–15 minutes, until smooth and elastic. Roll out on a floured cloth as thinly and evenly as possible until the weave of the cloth shows through.
- Rolling by machine: feed strips of dough repeatedly through the rollers, closing them one notch at a time to gradually thin the dough. This is time-consuming but necessary – resist the urge to skip a notch.

Cooking Pasta

- Use a pan that is large enough to allow the pasta to move around and swell.
- There is no need to add oil to the cooking water if you use enough water. Use 1 litre/1¾ pints water and 1 teaspoon salt for every 100 g/3½ oz pasta.
- Never cook more than 1 kg/2 lb 4 oz pasta in the same pan.

Making Polenta

- Dry polenta is poured into boiling salted water and stirred vigorously until the desired consistency is reached. Cooking times vary so always check the pack directions.
- Consistency depends on the ratio of water to polenta:
  Stiff: 2 parts water/1 part polenta.
  Medium: 5 parts water/1 part polenta.
  Soft: 7 parts water/1 part polenta.
- Stir in the polenta a handful at a time. To prevent lumps, make sure each handful is absorbed before adding the next. Polenta is cooked when it comes away from the sides of the pan.
- To serve wet: spoon into a serving dish.
- To serve dry: spread out in a shallow roasting tin and level with a wet palette knife. Leave until firm then slice into the desired shapes.
- To grill: place polenta slices in a grill pan and brush both sides with olive oil. Grill for 5–7 minutes, until golden and crisp at the edges. Turn and grill the other side.

Making Risotto

- Use a wide heavy-based pan.
- Do not wash risotto rice – the starch from the grains is an essential part of the dish.
- Make sure the stock is hot before you add it to the rice. It's best to keep it simmering in a small pan.
- Add a ladleful of cooking liquid at a time, and stir until the liquid disappears before adding the next.

Making Bread and Pizza Dough

- Always sift the flour first to remove any lumps and to incorporate air into the flour. Add the specified amount of salt to the flour when sifting, to distribute it evenly.
- Yeast thrives in warm surroundings. Make sure all the ingredients and equipment are warm before you begin.
- To make water tepid, use 1 part boiling to 2 parts cold.
- The amount of liquid needed may vary from the quantity stated in the recipe; it depends on the type of flour and the amount of moisture in the air. You need enough liquid to make the dough soft but not too sticky. Always keep back a little of the flour and water so you can adjust the consistency as necessary.
- Knead the dough for at least 10 minutes, until it feels silky smooth and springy.
- After kneading, leave the dough to rise in a lightly oiled deep bowl. Oiling allows the dough to rise smoothly without sticking to the sides of the bowl.
- Bake pizza at the highest possible temperature in the top of a preheated oven. Using a preheated pizza stone produces the crispest results. Otherwise use a perforated pizza pan – the holes allow heat and air to reach the centre of the base.

Antipasti and Soups

Antipasti have been part of Italian culture for centuries. Literally meaning 'before the meal' (from *pasto*, meaning 'meal'), the term refers to hot or cold appetizers served before the first course. Antipasti usually come in three categories – vegetable, meat and fish – and range from a simply prepared salad to more elaborate meat and seafood dishes. Some vegetables are served raw for dipping in a garlicky Bagna Calda; others are marinated in oil or pickled to accompany cured meats. There are seemingly endless varieties of cured meats with a wide range of textures and flavours. Some of the very best antipasti are made with fish and seafood. Crisp and succulent Pan-fried Prawns are one of the favourites, while economical fish such as fresh and dried anchovies and sardines appear in many guises.

Soups play an important part in Italian cuisine. They vary in consistency from light and delicate broths to main meal soups so hearty that you almost need a knife and fork to eat them. Soups are generally served warm in Italy rather than piping hot. Texture is always apparent – Italians rarely serve smooth soups. Some may be partially puréed but the identity of the ingredients is never entirely obliterated. There are regional characteristics too. In the north, soups are often based on rice, while tomato, garlic and pasta soups are typical of the south. Popular in Tuscany are thick bean- or bread-based soups, such as Bread and Tomato Soup or Ribollita, a hearty mixture of vegetables and beans with pieces of bread stirred into it. They are the perfect way to use up bread that has become slightly stale.

Bruschetta with Tomatoes

SERVES 4

300 g/10½ oz cherry tomatoes

4 sun-dried tomatoes

4 tbsp extra virgin olive oil

16 fresh basil leaves, shredded, plus extra
  leaves to garnish

8 slices ciabatta

2 garlic cloves, cut in half lengthways

salt and pepper

1. Using a sharp knife, cut the cherry tomatoes and sun-dried tomatoes in half. Place them in a bowl, add the oil and the shredded basil leaves and toss to mix well. Season to taste with salt and pepper.

2. Preheat the grill to medium, then lightly toast both sides of the ciabatta.

3. Rub the garlic, cut side down, over both sides of the toasted ciabatta bread.

4. Top the ciabatta with the tomato mixture and serve immediately, garnished with basil leaves.

Crostini alla Fiorentina

SERVES 6

3 tbsp olive oil
1 onion, chopped
1 celery stick, chopped
1 carrot, chopped
1–2 garlic cloves, crushed
125 g/4½ oz chicken livers
125 g/4½ oz calves', lambs' or pigs' liver
150 ml/5 fl oz red wine
1 tbsp tomato purée

2 tbsp chopped fresh flat-leaf parsley,
   plus extra sprigs to garnish
3–4 canned anchovy fillets, finely chopped
2 tbsp stock or water
25–40 g/1–1½ oz butter
1 tbsp capers, plus extra to garnish
12 slices ciabatta
salt and pepper

1. Heat the oil in a pan, add the onion, celery, carrot and garlic, and cook gently for 4–5 minutes, or until the onion is soft but not coloured.

2. Meanwhile, rinse and dry the chicken livers. Rinse and dry the calves' liver, and slice into strips. Add both types of liver to the pan and fry gently for a few minutes, until the strips are well sealed on all sides.

3. Add half the wine and cook until it has mostly evaporated. Then add the rest of the wine, the tomato purée, half the parsley, the anchovy fillets, stock or water, a little salt and plenty of black pepper.

4. Cover the pan and leave to simmer, stirring occasionally, for 15–20 minutes, or until tender and most of the liquid has been absorbed.

5. Leave the mixture to cool a little, then transfer to a food processor and process to a chunky purée.

6. Return the mixture to the pan and add the butter, capers and the remaining parsley. Heat through gently until the butter melts. Adjust the seasoning, adding salt and pepper if needed, and turn out into a bowl.

7. Preheat the grill to medium, then lightly toast both sides of the ciabatta. Spread the liver mixture, warm or cold, over the toasted ciabatta, garnish with parsley sprigs and capers, and serve.

Deep-fried Mozzarella Sandwiches

SERVES 4

8 slices bread, preferably slightly stale, crusts
   removed
100 g/3½ oz mozzarella cheese, sliced thickly
50 g/1¾ oz black olives, chopped
8 canned anchovy fillets, drained and chopped
16 fresh basil leaves, plus extra sprigs
   to garnish

4 eggs, beaten
150 ml/5 fl oz milk
oil, for deep-frying
salt and pepper

1. Cut each slice of bread into 2 triangles. Top 8 of the bread triangles with equal amounts of the
   mozzarella slices, olives and anchovies. Place the basil leaves on top and season with salt and
   pepper to taste. Lay the other 8 triangles of bread over the top and press down round the edges
   to seal.

2. Mix the eggs and milk together and pour into a wide, shallow baking dish. Add the sandwiches and
   leave to soak for about 5 minutes.

3. Heat enough oil for deep-frying in a large saucepan to 180–190°C/350–375°F, or until a cube of
   bread browns in 30 seconds. Before cooking the sandwiches, squeeze the edges together again.

4. Carefully place the sandwiches in the oil and deep-fry for 2 minutes, or until golden, turning once.
   (You will have to cook them in batches.) Remove with a slotted spoon and drain on kitchen paper.
   Serve immediately garnished with basil sprigs.

Aubergine Rolls

SERVES 4

2 aubergines, thinly sliced lengthways
5 tbsp olive oil
1 garlic clove, crushed
4 tbsp pesto

175 g/6 oz grated mozzarella cheese
small bunch fresh basil leaves, torn, plus extra
   sprigs to garnish
salt and pepper

1. Preheat the oven to 180°C/350°F/Gas Mark 4. Sprinkle the aubergine slices liberally with salt and leave to stand for 10–15 minutes to extract the bitter juices. Turn the slices over and repeat. Rinse well with cold water and drain on kitchen paper.

2. Heat the oil in a large frying pan and add the garlic. Fry the aubergine slices lightly on both sides, a few at a time. Drain on kitchen paper.

3. Spread the pesto onto one side of the aubergine slices. Top with the mozzarella and sprinkle with the torn basil leaves. Season with a little salt and pepper. Roll up the slices and secure with wooden cocktail sticks.

4. Arrange the aubergine rolls in a greased ovenproof baking dish. Place in the preheated oven and bake for 8–10 minutes.

5. Transfer the aubergine rolls to a warmed serving plate. Garnish with basil sprigs and serve immediately.

Marinated Mushrooms

SERVES 6–8

1 kg/2 lb 4 oz mixed mushrooms, such as ceps,
  chanterelles, oyster mushrooms and/or
  chestnut mushrooms
1 fresh red chilli

250 ml/9 fl oz olive oil
100 ml/3½ fl oz white balsamic vinegar
fresh rosemary or oregano sprigs
salt

1. Wipe the mushrooms with damp kitchen paper. Cut the chilli in half lengthways and remove the seeds, then cut into thin strips. Set aside.

2. Heat 5 tablespoons of the oil in a large saucepan, then add the mushrooms and cook, stirring, until all the juices have evaporated. Add the reserved chilli strips and cook, stirring, for a further 1–2 minutes. Stir in the vinegar and season to taste with salt.

3. Tip the contents of the saucepan into a bowl, then stir in the rosemary sprigs and pour over the remaining oil. Cover with clingfilm and leave to marinate in the refrigerator overnight before serving.

Marinated White Beans

SERVES 4

250 g/9 oz dried cannellini beans
1 bay leaf
1 garlic clove
4 spring onions
1 tbsp lemon juice

3 tbsp white wine vinegar
5 tbsp olive oil
salt and pepper
chopped fresh parsley and Parmesan cheese
shavings, to serve

1. Place the beans in a large bowl, cover with plenty of water and leave to soak overnight.

2. Pour the beans with their soaking water into a saucepan, add the bay leaf and whole garlic clove and bring to the boil. Reduce the heat and simmer gently, occasionally skimming off any scum, for 1–1½ hours, or until the beans are tender.

3. Remove from the heat and discard the bay leaf and garlic. Leave the beans to cool in the cooking water until lukewarm. Meanwhile, cut the spring onions into thin strips and set aside. Mix the lemon juice, vinegar and oil in a bowl with salt and pepper to taste to make a dressing.

4. Pour the beans into a colander and drain well. Transfer to a large serving bowl, stir in the spring onions and dressing and leave to marinate for at least 15 minutes. Scatter over the parsley and Parmesan shavings just before serving.

Sun-dried Tomato Bagna Calda with Spring Vegetables

SERVES 4

800 g/1 lb 12 oz prepared mixed spring
vegetables, such as celery sticks, asparagus
spears, broccoli florets and artichoke hearts

country-style bread, cut into bite-sized cubes,
toasted if preferred

BAGNA CALDA

200 ml/7 fl oz extra virgin olive oil

3 garlic cloves, thinly sliced

50 g/1 ¾ oz canned anchovy fillets in olive oil,
drained

1 tbsp unsalted butter (optional)

3–4 sun-dried tomatoes in oil, drained and very
finely chopped

4–5 fresh basil leaves, torn

1. Lightly cook vegetables separately in boiling water until just tender. Drain and leave to cool.

2. Arrange all the vegetables on a serving plate with the bread cubes. Alternatively, serve the bread cubes in a separate little basket or dish.

3. To make the bagna calda, put the oil, garlic and anchovies in a saucepan over a low heat. Mash the anchovies with a fork and heat, stirring, for 3–4 minutes, until they have started to melt into the oil and the garlic slices have softened. Be careful to avoid letting the mixture become too hot, or the garlic will simply fry and the mixture will be ruined. Stir in the butter, if using, and the sun-dried tomatoes.

4. Transfer the mixture to a small serving bowl and stir in the basil. Serve immediately with the prepared vegetables and bread cubes.

Mixed Antipasto Meat Platter

SERVES 4

1 cantaloupe melon
55 g/2 oz Italian salami, thinly sliced
8 slices prosciutto
8 slices bresaola
8 slices mortadella
4 plum tomatoes, thinly sliced
4 fresh figs, halved

115 g/4 oz black olives, pitted
2 tbsp shredded fresh basil leaves
4 tbsp extra virgin olive oil, plus extra
   for serving
pepper
ciabatta, to serve

1. Cut the melon in half and scoop out and discard the seeds, then cut the flesh into 8 wedges. Arrange the wedges on one end of a large serving platter.

2. Arrange the salami, prosciutto, bresaola and mortadella in loose folds on the other end of the platter. Arrange the tomato slices and fig halves along the centre of the platter.

3. Sprinkle the olives and shredded basil over the platter and drizzle with oil. Season to taste with pepper, then serve with ciabatta and extra oil for dipping and drizzling.

Beef Carpaccio

SERVES 4

200 g/7 oz beef tenderloin, in one piece
2 tbsp lemon juice
4 tbsp extra virgin olive oil
55 g/2 oz Parmesan cheese shavings

4 tbsp chopped fresh flat-leaf parsley
salt and pepper
lemon wedges, to garnish
fresh bread, to serve

1. Using a sharp knife, cut the beef into wafer-thin slices and arrange on 4 individual serving plates.

2. Pour the lemon juice into a small bowl and season to taste with salt and pepper. Stir in the oil, then pour the dressing over the meat. Cover the plates with clingfilm and set aside for 10–15 minutes to marinate.

3. Remove and discard the clingfilm. Arrange the Parmesan shavings in the centre of each serving and sprinkle with parsley. Garnish with lemon wedges and serve with fresh bread.

Pan-fried Prawns

SERVES 4

4 garlic cloves
20–24 unshelled large raw prawns
125 g/4½ oz butter
4 tbsp olive oil
6 tbsp brandy

salt and pepper
2 tbsp chopped fresh flat-leaf parsley,
  to garnish
lemon wedges, to serve

1. Using a sharp knife, peel and slice the garlic. Wash the prawns and pat dry using kitchen paper.

2. Melt the butter with the oil in a large frying pan, add the garlic and prawns, and fry over a high heat, stirring, for 3–4 minutes, until the prawns are pink.

3. Sprinkle with the brandy and season to taste with salt and pepper. Garnish with parsley and serve immediately with lemon wedges for squeezing over.

Pan-fried Whole Sardines

SERVES 4

500 g/1 lb 2 oz small fresh sardines, scaled
plain flour, for dusting

olive oil, for shallow-frying
coarse sea salt and lemon wedges, to serve

1. Wash the sardines and pat dry with kitchen paper. If the sardines are longer than 9 cm/3½ inches, remove the heads and gut them. Smaller fish may be cooked whole.

2. Spread out the flour on a plate and use to coat the sardines, tapping off any excess.

3. Heat 4 cm/1½ inches of oil in a frying pan and cook the sardines over a medium–high heat until golden brown. Transfer to a serving plate, sprinkle with sea salt and serve with lemon wedges for squeezing over.

Vegetable Soup with Pesto

SERVES 6

1 tbsp olive oil
1 onion, finely chopped
1 large leek, thinly sliced
1 celery stick, thinly sliced
1 carrot, quartered and thinly sliced
1 garlic clove, finely chopped
1.5 litres/2½ pints water
1 potato, diced
1 parsnip, finely diced
1 small kohlrabi or turnip, diced
150 g/5½ oz green beans,
  cut in small pieces
150 g/5½ oz fresh or frozen peas

2 small courgettes, quartered lengthways and
  sliced
400 g/14 oz canned flageolet beans, drained
  and rinsed
100 g/3½ oz spinach leaves, cut into thin
  ribbons
salt and pepper

PESTO
1 large garlic clove, very finely chopped
15 g/½ oz fresh basil leaves
75 g/2¾ oz Parmesan cheese, grated
4 tbsp extra virgin olive oil

1. Heat the olive oil in a large saucepan over a low–medium heat. Add the onion and leek and cook
    for 5 minutes, stirring occasionally, until the onion softens. Add the celery, carrot and garlic and
    cook, covered, for a further 5 minutes, stirring frequently.

2. Add the water, potato, parsnip, kohlrabi and green beans. Bring to the boil, reduce the heat to low
    and simmer, covered, for 5 minutes.

3. Add the peas, courgettes and flageolet beans, and season generously with salt and pepper. Cover
    again and simmer for about 25 minutes, until all the vegetables are tender.

4. Meanwhile, make the pesto. Put the garlic, basil and Parmesan in a food processor with the olive
    oil and process until smooth, scraping down the sides as necessary. Alternatively, pound together
    using a pestle and mortar.

5. Add the spinach to the soup and simmer for a further 5 minutes. Taste and adjust the seasoning,
    adding salt and pepper if needed, and stir about a tablespoon of the pesto into the soup. Ladle
    into warmed bowls and serve with the remaining pesto.

Bread and Tomato Soup

SERVES 6

450 g/1 lb two-day-old crusty Italian open-textured bread, such as Pugliese

1 kg/2 lb 4 oz ripe plum tomatoes

4 tbsp olive oil

4 garlic cloves, crushed

500 ml/18 fl oz boiling water

1 bunch fresh basil

salt and pepper

6 tbsp extra virgin olive oil, to serve

1. Cut the bread into slices and then cubes (you can remove some of the crusts if you want) and leave to dry out for 30 minutes. Meanwhile, peel the tomatoes and cut them into chunks.

2. Heat the olive oil in a large saucepan, add the garlic and cook over a medium heat, stirring, for 1 minute without browning. Add the tomatoes and simmer gently for 20–30 minutes, until the mixture has thickened.

3. Add the bread and stir until it has absorbed the liquid. Stir in the boiling water until you have a thick soupy mixture. Season to taste with salt and pepper.

4. Remove the basil leaves from their stems and tear any large leaves into pieces. Stir the basil into the soup.

5. Serve warm with a tablespoonful of extra virgin olive oil sprinkled over each bowl.

Ribollita

SERVES 4

3 tbsp olive oil

2 red onions, roughly chopped

3 carrots, sliced

3 celery sticks, roughly chopped

3 garlic cloves, chopped

1 tbsp chopped fresh thyme

400 g/14 oz canned cannellini beans, drained and rinsed

400 g/14 oz canned chopped tomatoes

600 ml/1 pint water or vegetable stock

2 tbsp chopped fresh parsley

500 g/1 lb 2 oz cavolo nero or savoy cabbage, trimmed and sliced

1 small day-old ciabatta loaf, torn into small pieces

salt and pepper

extra virgin olive oil, to serve

1. Heat the olive oil in a large saucepan and cook the onions, carrots and celery for 10–15 minutes, stirring frequently. Add the garlic, thyme and salt and pepper to taste. Continue to cook for a further 1–2 minutes, until the vegetables are golden and caramelized.

2. Add the beans to the pan and pour in the tomatoes. Add enough of the water to cover the vegetables. Bring to the boil and simmer for 20 minutes. Add the parsley and cavolo nero and cook for a further 5 minutes.

3. Stir in the bread and add a little more water, if needed. The soup should be thick.

4. Taste and adjust the seasoning, adding salt and pepper if needed. Ladle into warmed serving bowls and serve immediately, drizzled with extra virgin olive oil.

Tuscan Bean Soup

SERVES 6

300 g/10½ oz canned cannellini beans, drained
and rinsed

300 g/10½ oz canned borlotti beans, drained
and rinsed

600 ml/1 pint chicken or vegetable stock

115 g/4 oz dried conchigliette or other small
pasta shapes

4 tbsp olive oil

2 garlic cloves, finely chopped

3 tbsp chopped fresh flat-leaf parsley

salt and pepper

1. Place half the cannellini beans and half the borlotti beans in a food processor with half the stock and process until smooth. Pour into a large, heavy-based saucepan and add the remaining beans. Stir in enough of the remaining stock to achieve the consistency you like, then bring to the boil.

2. Add the pasta and return to the boil, then reduce the heat and cook for 15 minutes, or until just tender.

3. Meanwhile, heat 3 tablespoons of the oil in a small frying pan. Add the garlic and cook, stirring constantly, for 2–3 minutes, or until golden. Stir the garlic into the soup with the parsley.

4. Season to taste with salt and pepper and ladle into warmed soup bowls. Drizzle with the remaining oil to taste and serve immediately.

First Course

The first course (*primo piatto*) of an Italian meal usually comprises a grain-based dish: pasta, gnocchi, risotto or polenta. Pasta is universally popular – easy to cook and wonderfully versatile. It is served in soups, with a variety of sauces, or stuffed and baked in the oven. Some of the best-known pasta dishes are made with long strands or ribbons combined with a hearty sauce. Spaghetti Bolognese and Spaghetti alla Carbonara are well-known classics, but there are other sauces worth trying – fiery tomato-based *arrabbiata*, for example, or the robust *puttanesca* with tomatoes, capers, olives and anchovies. Delicately stuffed ravioli squares with a simple herb butter sauce are also good as a first course, as are Spinach Cannelloni or Lasagne al Forno.

Gnocchi are feather-light, tiny dumplings made with mashed potato and flour, or flour on its own, often flavoured with spinach or some sort

of cheese. They are cooked in boiling water and served with various sauces or melted cheese and butter.

All types of risotto are served as a first course, particularly in northern Italy where rice is a major crop. Risotto is made with short-grain rice, which is characteristically creamier than long-grain rice. Parmesan cheese is a key ingredient in risotto, except those containing fish or seafood, and is stirred in just before serving.

Polenta is also popular in northern Italy. It is made with cornmeal and water, and is served either as a soft porridge or a firmer cake that is fried until crisp. In the north-central region, polenta is usually served soft and creamy, often infused with cheese. Further east you are more likely to find it fried or grilled.

Spaghetti Bolognese

SERVES 4

1 tbsp olive oil

1 onion, finely chopped

2 garlic cloves, chopped

1 carrot, chopped

1 celery stick, chopped

50 g/1¾ oz pancetta or streaky bacon, diced

350 g/12 oz fresh lean beef mince

400 g/14 oz canned chopped tomatoes

2 tsp dried oregano

125 ml/4 fl oz red wine

2 tbsp tomato purée

350 g/12 oz dried spaghetti

salt and pepper

fresh Parmesan cheese shavings, to serve

1. Heat the oil in a large frying pan. Add the onion and cook for 3 minutes, until softened. Add the garlic, carrot, celery and pancetta and sauté for 3–4 minutes, or until just beginning to brown.

2. Add the beef and cook over a high heat for a further 3 minutes, or until all of the meat is browned. Stir in the tomatoes, oregano and wine and bring to the boil. Reduce the heat and leave to simmer for about 45 minutes. Stir in the tomato purée and season to taste with salt and pepper.

3. Meanwhile, bring a large saucepan of lightly salted water to the boil. Add the pasta, return to the boil and cook for 8–10 minutes, or until tender but still firm to the bite. Drain thoroughly.

4. Transfer the spaghetti to a serving plate and pour over the bolognese sauce. Toss to mix well and serve with Parmesan cheese shavings.

Spaghetti alla Carbonara

SERVES 4

400 g/14 oz dried spaghetti
4 eggs
4 tbsp double cream
50 g/1¾ oz Parmesan cheese, grated

50 g/1¾ oz pecorino cheese, grated
1 tbsp butter
150 g/5½ oz pancetta, diced
salt and pepper

1. Bring a large saucepan of lightly salted water to the boil. Add the pasta, return to the boil and cook for 8–10 minutes, or until tender but still firm to the bite.

2. Meanwhile, beat the eggs in a bowl with the cream, cheeses and salt and pepper to taste. Melt the butter in a large frying pan and cook the pancetta until crispy.

3. Drain the pasta, but not too thoroughly, then add to the frying pan and pour over the egg mixture. Remove from the heat and stir until the egg mixture is warmed through but still creamy.

4. Transfer to warmed serving plates and sprinkle with freshly ground black pepper. Serve immediately.

Pasta Arrabbiata

SERVES 4

150 ml/5 fl oz dry white wine
1 tbsp sun-dried tomato purée
2 fresh red chillies
2 garlic cloves, finely chopped
350 g/12 oz dried tortiglioni
4 tbsp chopped fresh flat-leaf parsley
salt and pepper
fresh pecorino cheese shavings, to garnish

SUGOCASA
5 tbsp extra virgin olive oil
450 g/1 lb plum tomatoes, chopped
salt and pepper

1. To make the sugocasa, heat the oil in a frying pan over a high heat until almost smoking. Add the tomatoes and cook, stirring frequently, for 2–3 minutes. Reduce the heat to low and cook gently for 20 minutes, or until soft. Season to taste with salt and pepper. Using a wooden spoon, press through a non-metallic sieve into a saucepan.

2. Add the wine, tomato purée, whole chillies and garlic to the sugocasa and bring to the boil. Reduce the heat and simmer gently.

3. Meanwhile, bring a large saucepan of lightly salted water to the boil. Add the pasta, return to the boil and cook for 8–10 minutes, or until the pasta is tender but still firm to the bite.

4. Remove the chillies and taste the sauce. If you prefer a hotter flavour, chop some or all of the chillies and return to the saucepan. Check and adjust the seasoning, adding salt and pepper, if needed, then stir in half the parsley.

5. Drain the pasta and transfer to a warmed serving bowl. Add the sauce and toss to coat. Sprinkle with the remaining parsley, garnish with the cheese shavings and serve at once.

Tagliatelle with Pesto

SERVES 4

450 g/1 lb dried tagliatelle
salt

BASIL PESTO
2 garlic cloves
25 g/1 oz pine kernels
115 g/4 oz fresh basil leaves, plus extra
  to garnish
125 ml/4 fl oz olive oil
55 g/2 oz freshly grated Parmesan cheese
salt

1. To make the basil pesto, put the garlic and pine kernels into a food processor or blender and process briefly. Add the basil leaves and process to a paste. With the motor still running, gradually add the oil. Scrape into a bowl and beat in the Parmesan cheese. Season to taste with salt. Alternatively, pound together using a mortar and pestle.

2. Bring a large saucepan of lightly salted water to the boil. Add the pasta, return to the boil and cook for 8–10 minutes, or until tender but still firm to the bite. Drain well, return to the saucepan and toss with half the pesto.

3. Divide between warmed serving plates and top with the remaining pesto. Garnish with the basil leaves and serve.

Spaghetti alla Norma

SERVES 4

175 ml/6 fl oz olive oil

500 g/1 lb 2 oz plum tomatoes, peeled and chopped

1 garlic clove, chopped

350 g/12 oz aubergines, diced

400 g/14 oz dried spaghetti

½ bunch fresh basil, torn

115 g/4 oz freshly grated pecorino cheese

salt and pepper

1. Heat 4 tablespoons of the oil in a large saucepan. Add the tomatoes and garlic, season to taste with salt and pepper, cover and cook over a low heat, stirring occasionally, for 25 minutes.

2. Meanwhile, heat the remaining oil in a heavy-based frying pan. Add the aubergines and cook, stirring occasionally, for 5 minutes, until evenly golden brown. Remove with a slotted spoon and drain on kitchen paper.

3. Bring a large pan of salted water to the boil. Add the pasta, return to the boil and cook for 8–10 minutes, or until tender but still firm to the bite.

4. Meanwhile, stir the drained aubergines into the tomato mixture. Taste and adjust the seasoning, adding salt and pepper if needed.

5. Drain the pasta and place in a warmed serving dish. Add the tomato and aubergine mixture, basil and half the pecorino cheese. Toss well, sprinkle with the remaining cheese and serve immediately.

Spaghetti alla Puttanesca

SERVES 4

3 tbsp olive oil

2 garlic cloves, finely chopped

10 canned anchovy fillets, drained and
  chopped

140 g/5 oz black olives, stoned and chopped

1 tbsp capers, drained and rinsed

450 g/1 lb plum tomatoes, peeled, deseeded
  and chopped

pinch of cayenne pepper

400 g/14 oz dried spaghetti

salt

2 tbsp chopped fresh flat-leaf parsley,
  to garnish

1. Heat the oil in a heavy-based frying pan. Add the garlic and cook over a low heat, stirring
   frequently, for 2 minutes. Add the anchovies and mash them to a pulp with a fork. Add the olives,
   capers and tomatoes and season to taste with cayenne pepper. Cover and simmer for 25 minutes.

2. Meanwhile, bring a large saucepan of lightly salted water to the boil. Add the pasta, return to the
   boil and cook for 8–10 minutes, or until tender but still firm to the bite. Drain well and transfer to a
   warmed serving dish.

3. Spoon the anchovy sauce into the dish and toss the pasta, using 2 large forks. Garnish with the
   chopped parsley and serve immediately.

Spaghetti con Vongole

SERVES 4

1 kg/2 lb 4 oz clams, scrubbed
175 ml/6 fl oz water
175 ml/6 fl oz dry white wine
350 g/12 oz dried spaghetti

5 tbsp olive oil
2 garlic cloves, finely chopped
4 tbsp chopped fresh flat-leaf parsley
salt and pepper

1. Discard any clams with broken shells and any that refuse to close when tapped. Place the clams in a large heavy-based saucepan. Add the water and wine, then cover and cook over a high heat, shaking the saucepan occasionally, for 5 minutes, or until the shells have opened. Remove the clams with a slotted spoon and strain the liquid through a muslin-lined sieve into a small saucepan. Bring to the boil and cook until reduced by about half. Discard any clams that remain closed and remove the remainder from their shells.

2. Bring a large saucepan of lightly salted water to the boil. Add the pasta, return to the boil and cook for 8–10 minutes, or until tender but still firm to the bite.

3. Meanwhile, heat the oil in a large heavy-based frying pan. Add the garlic and cook, stirring frequently, for 2 minutes. Add the parsley and the reduced cooking liquid and simmer gently. Drain the pasta and add it to the frying pan with the clams. Season to taste with salt and pepper and cook, stirring constantly, for 4 minutes, or until the pasta is coated and the clams have heated through. Transfer to a warmed serving dish and serve immediately.

Sweet Potato Ravioli with Sage Butter

SERVES 4

PASTA
400 g/14 oz type '00' pasta flour or plain flour
4 eggs, beaten
semolina, for dusting
salt

FILLING
500 g/1 lb 2 oz sweet potatoes
3 tbsp olive oil
1 large onion, finely chopped

1 garlic clove, crushed
1 tsp chopped fresh thyme leaves
2 tbsp honey
salt and pepper

SAGE BUTTER
50 g/1¾ oz butter
1 bunch chopped fresh sage leaves, reserving a
   few leaves to garnish

1. To make the pasta, sift the flour into a large bowl or food processor. Add the eggs and bring the mixture together or process to make a soft but not sticky dough. Turn out onto a work surface lightly dusted with semolina and knead for 4–5 minutes, until smooth. Cover with clingfilm and leave to chill in the refrigerator for at least 30 minutes.

2. For the filling, peel the sweet potatoes and cut into chunks. Cook in a saucepan of boiling water for 20 minutes, or until tender. Drain and mash. Heat the oil in a frying pan over a medium heat, add the onion and cook, stirring frequently, for 4–5 minutes, until softened but not coloured. Stir the onion into the mashed potatoes and add the garlic and thyme leaves. Drizzle with the honey and season to taste with salt and pepper. Set aside.

3. Using a pasta machine or rolling pan, roll the pasta out to a thickness of about 1 mm/1⁄32 inch. Cut the pasta in half. Place teaspoonfuls of the filling at evenly spaced intervals across one half of the pasta. Brush around the filling with a small amount of water and cover with the second half of the pasta. Press lightly around the filling to seal the pasta and cut into squares with a sharp knife or pastry wheel. Lay the ravioli out on a sheet of greaseproof paper that has been lightly dusted with semolina.

4. Bring a large saucepan of lightly salted water to the boil. Add the ravioli, return to the boil and cook for 2–3 minutes, or until the pasta rises to the surface and is tender but still firm to the bite.

5. Meanwhile, for the sage butter, melt the butter with the sage in a small saucepan over a low heat.

6. Drain the ravioli and toss with the sage butter. Serve immediately, garnished with sage leaves.

Lasagne al Forno

SERVES 4

2 tbsp olive oil
55 g/2 oz pancetta, chopped
1 onion, chopped
1 garlic clove, finely chopped
225 g/8 oz fresh beef mince
2 celery sticks, chopped
2 carrots, chopped
pinch of sugar
½ tsp dried oregano
400 g/14 oz canned chopped tomatoes
8 oz/225 g dried no-precook lasagne sheets

115 g/4 oz grated Parmesan cheese
salt and pepper

CHEESE SAUCE
25 g/1 oz butter
25 g/1 oz plain flour
300 ml/10 fl oz warm milk
140 g/5 oz Cheddar cheese, grated
2 tsp Dijon mustard
salt and pepper

1. Preheat the oven to 190°C/375°F/Gas Mark 5. Heat the oil in a large heavy-based saucepan.
    Add the pancetta and cook over a medium heat, stirring occasionally, for 3 minutes, or until the
    fat begins to run. Add the onion and garlic and cook, stirring occasionally, for 5 minutes, or until
    softened.

2. Add the beef and cook, breaking it up with a wooden spoon, until browned all over. Stir in the
    celery and carrots and cook for 5 minutes. Season to taste with salt and pepper. Add the sugar,
    oregano and tomatoes and their can juices. Bring to the boil, reduce the heat and simmer for
    30 minutes.

3. Meanwhile, make the cheese sauce. Melt the butter in a saucepan. Add the flour and cook over
    a low heat, stirring constantly, for 2 minutes. Remove the pan from the heat and gradually stir in
    the milk. Return the pan to a low heat and bring to the boil, stirring constantly. Continue to cook,
    stirring constantly, until thickened and smooth. Stir in the Cheddar cheese until it melts and add the
    mustard. Season to taste with salt and pepper.

4. In a large, rectangular ovenproof dish, make alternate layers of meat sauce, lasagne sheets and
    Parmesan cheese. Pour the cheese sauce over the layers, covering them completely, and sprinkle
    with the remaining Parmesan cheese. Bake in the preheated oven for 30 minutes, or until golden
    brown and bubbling. Serve immediately.

Spinach Cannelloni

SERVES 4

oil, for greasing
600 g/1 lb 5 oz spinach
25 g/1 oz butter
1 small onion, finely chopped
200 g/7 oz ricotta cheese
½ tsp freshly grated nutmeg
12 dried cannelloni tubes
50 g/1¾ oz Parmesan cheese, grated
salt and pepper

BÉCHAMEL SAUCE
600 ml/1 pint milk
1 bay leaf
6 black peppercorns
slice of onion
blade of mace
55 g/2 oz butter
55 g/2 oz plain flour
salt and pepper

1. Preheat the oven to 200°C/400°F/Gas Mark 6. Oil a large, rectangular baking dish.

2. To make the béchamel sauce, pour the milk into a saucepan and add the bay leaf, peppercorns, onion and mace. Bring to just below boiling point, then remove from the heat and leave to infuse for 10 minutes. Strain the milk into a jug, discarding the seasonings. Melt the butter in a clean pan. Add the flour and cook over a low heat, stirring constantly, for 2 minutes. Remove the pan from the heat and gradually stir in the flavoured milk. Return the pan to a low heat and bring to the boil, stirring constantly. Simmer, stirring constantly, until thickened and smooth. Season to taste with salt and pepper.

3. Remove and discard any tough stems from the spinach, then place the leaves in a colander and wash under cold running water. Leave to drain.

4. Melt the butter in a large saucepan over a medium heat and cook the onion for 4–5 minutes, until softened and translucent. Stir in the spinach, with the water still clinging to its leaves, cover and cook for a further 3–4 minutes, until wilted.

5. Transfer the spinach and onion mixture to a sieve and leave to drain, then squeeze out as much water as possible. Chop the spinach, then transfer to a bowl with the ricotta cheese, nutmeg and salt and pepper to taste. Mix well and set aside.

6. Spoon the spinach mixture into a piping bag fitted with a large, plain nozzle and use to fill the cannelloni tubes. Place the filled cannelloni tubes in the prepared baking dish, pour over the béchamel sauce and sprinkle with the Parmesan cheese. Bake in the preheated oven for 25–30 minutes. Serve immediately.

Potato Gnocchi with Walnut Pesto

SERVES 4

450 g/1 lb floury potatoes
55 g/2 oz Parmesan cheese, freshly grated
1 egg, beaten
200 g/7 oz plain flour, plus extra
   for dusting
salt and pepper

WALNUT PESTO
40 g/1½ oz fresh flat-leaf parsley
2 tbsp capers, rinsed
2 garlic cloves
175 ml/6 fl oz extra virgin olive oil
70 g/2½ oz walnut halves
40 g/1½ oz pecorino or Parmesan cheese,
   freshly grated
salt and pepper

1. Boil the potatoes in their skins in a large saucepan of water for 30–35 minutes, until tender. Drain well and leave to cool slightly.

2. Meanwhile, to make the walnut pesto, chop the parsley, capers and garlic, then put in a mortar with the oil, walnuts and salt and pepper to taste. Pound with a pestle to a coarse paste. Add the pecorino cheese and stir well.

3. When the potatoes are cool enough to handle, peel off the skins and pass the flesh through a sieve into a large bowl or press through a potato ricer. While still hot, season well with salt and pepper and add the Parmesan cheese. Beat in the egg and sift in the flour. Lightly mix together, then turn out onto a lightly floured work surface. Knead lightly until the mixture becomes a smooth dough. If it is too sticky, add a little more flour.

4. Roll the dough out with your hands into a long log. Cut into 2.5-cm/1-inch pieces and gently press with a fork to give the traditional ridged effect. Transfer to a floured baking sheet and cover with a clean tea towel while you make the remaining gnocchi.

5. Bring a large saucepan of lightly salted water to the boil. Carefully add the gnocchi, in small batches, return to the boil and cook for 2–3 minutes, or until they rise to the surface. Remove with a slotted spoon and transfer to a warmed serving dish to keep warm while you cook the remaining gnocchi.

6. Serve the gnocchi in warmed serving bowls with a good spoonful of the pesto on top.

Spinach and Ricotta Gnocchi

SERVES 4–6

1 tbsp olive oil

500 g/1 lb 2 oz spinach leaves

225 g/8 oz ricotta cheese

115 g/4 oz Parmesan or pecorino cheese, freshly grated

2 eggs, lightly beaten

55 g/2 oz plain flour, plus extra for dusting

freshly grated nutmeg

salt and pepper

SAUCE

2 tbsp olive oil

2 shallots, finely chopped

1 carrot, finely diced

2 garlic cloves, crushed

800 g/1 lb 12 oz canned chopped tomatoes

1 tbsp tomato purée

6 fresh basil leaves, roughly torn into pieces, plus extra to garnish

salt and pepper

1. Heat the oil in a large saucepan. Add the spinach and cook, covered, for 1–2 minutes, until just wilted. Drain through a sieve and leave to cool, then squeeze out as much moisture as possible.

2. Finely chop the spinach and put it in a bowl. Add the ricotta cheese, half the Parmesan cheese, the eggs and flour and mix well. Season to taste with salt and pepper and add a good grating of nutmeg. Cover and leave to chill in the refrigerator for at least 1 hour.

3. Meanwhile, make the sauce. Heat the oil in a saucepan, add the shallots, carrot and garlic, and cook over a medium heat, stirring frequently, for 3–4 minutes, until soft. Add the tomatoes and tomato purée and bring to the boil, then reduce the heat and simmer, uncovered, for 10–15 minutes, until the sauce is reduced and thickened. Season to taste with salt and pepper and add the basil. If you like a smooth sauce, pass it through a sieve or process in a food processor or blender.

4. To shape the gnocchi, flour your hands thoroughly. Put a dessertspoonful of the spinach mixture into the palm of one hand, roll gently into an egg shape and transfer to a floured baking sheet. Repeat with the remaining spinach mixture.

5. Bring a large saucepan of lightly salted water to the boil. Carefully add the gnocchi, in small batches, return to the boil and cook for 2–3 minutes, or until they rise to the surface. Remove with a slotted spoon and transfer to a warmed serving dish to keep warm while you cook the remaining gnocchi.

6. Transfer the gnocchi to individual serving dishes and top with the sauce. Sprinkle over the remaining Parmesan cheese, garnish with basil and serve immediately.

Baked Polenta with Cheese and Thyme

SERVES 4

600 ml/1 pint water
600 ml/1 pint milk
1 tsp sea salt
½ tsp freshly grated nutmeg
300 g/10½ oz fine polenta
25g/1 oz Parmesan cheese, finely grated

150 g/5½ oz Gruyère cheese, diced
50 g/1¾ oz unsalted butter, plus extra
  for greasing
2 fresh thyme sprigs, leaves only
pepper
salad leaves, to serve

1. Put the water and milk in a large saucepan and bring to the boil over a high heat. Add the salt, nutmeg and pepper to taste, then pour in the polenta, stirring constantly. Reduce the heat to medium and cook, stirring constantly, for a further 25–30 minutes, or until the polenta is thick and coming away from the sides of the pan.

2. Remove from the heat and add the Parmesan cheese and half the Gruyère cheese and butter. Stir until melted and well combined.

3. Pour the polenta onto a non-stick baking tray, then spread out to a thickness of 1 cm/½ inch and leave to cool completely.

4. Preheat the oven to 200°C/400°F/Gas Mark 6. Grease a shallow baking dish.

5. Using a plain biscuit cutter, stamp out 5-cm/2-inch rounds of the polenta and arrange, overlapping, in the prepared baking dish. Dice the remaining butter and scatter over the polenta rounds with the remaining Gruyère cheese and the thyme leaves.

6. Bake in the preheated oven for 15 minutes, until golden and crisp. Serve with salad leaves.

Risotto Primavera

SERVES 4

1.5 litres/2¾ pints chicken or vegetable stock

225 g/8 oz fine asparagus spears

4 tbsp olive oil

175 g/6 oz young French beans, cut into
2.5-cm/1-inch lengths

175 g/6 oz young courgettes, quartered and
cut into 2.5-cm/1-inch lengths

225 g/8 oz shelled fresh peas

1 onion, finely chopped

1–2 garlic cloves, finely chopped

350 g/12 oz risotto rice

4 spring onions, cut into 2.5-cm/1-inch lengths

4 tbsp butter

115 g/4 oz grated Parmesan cheese

2 tbsp snipped fresh chives

2 tbsp shredded fresh basil

salt and pepper

1. Bring the stock to the boil in a saucepan, then reduce the heat and keep simmering gently over a
   low heat while you are cooking the risotto.

2. Trim the woody ends of the asparagus and cut off the tips. Cut the stems into 2.5-cm/1-in pieces
   and set aside with the tips.

3. Heat 2 tablespoons of the oil in a large frying pan over a high heat until hot. Add the asparagus,
   beans, courgettes and peas and stir-fry for 3–4 minutes, until they are bright green and just
   beginning to soften. Set aside.

4. Heat the remaining oil in a large, heavy-based saucepan over a medium heat. Add the onion and
   cook, stirring occasionally, for 3 minutes, or until it begins to soften. Stir in the garlic and cook, while
   stirring, for 30 seconds.

5. Reduce the heat, add the rice and mix to coat in oil. Cook, stirring constantly, for 2–3 minutes,
   or until the grains are translucent.

6. Gradually add the hot stock, a ladleful at a time. Stir constantly and add more liquid as the rice
   absorbs each addition. Cook for 20 minutes, or until all but 2 tablespoons of the liquid has been
   absorbed and the rice is creamy but still firm to the bite.

7. Stir in the stir-fried vegetables and spring onions with the remaining stock. Cook for 2 minutes,
   stirring frequently, then season to taste with salt and pepper. Stir in the butter, Parmesan cheese,
   chives and basil. Remove the saucepan from the heat. Transfer the risotto to warmed serving dishes
   and serve immediately.

Mushroom Risotto

SERVES 4

55 g/2 oz dried porcini

250 ml/9 fl oz warm water

700 ml/1¼ pints hot chicken stock

6 tbsp olive oil

280 g/10 oz mixed fresh wild or field
  mushrooms, thickly sliced

2 garlic cloves, finely chopped

1 tbsp finely chopped fresh thyme

1 onion, finely chopped

350 g/12 oz risotto rice

150 ml/5 fl oz dry white wine

55 g/2 oz butter

115 g/4 oz Parmesan cheese

salt and pepper

2 tbsp finely chopped fresh flat-leaf parsley,
  to garnish

1. Soak the dried mushrooms in the warm water in a small bowl for 10–15 minutes. Drain, reserving the soaking liquid (strain it thoroughly to remove any grit). Finely slice the drained mushrooms.

2. Bring the stock to a boil in a saucepan, then reduce the heat and keep simmering gently over a low heat while you are cooking the risotto.

3. Heat half the oil in a large frying pan, add the fresh mushrooms and cook over a low heat, stirring occasionally, for 10–15 minutes, or until softened. Add the dried mushrooms and garlic and cook, stirring frequently, for a further 2–3 minutes. Add the thyme and salt and pepper to taste, then remove the mushroom mixture from the frying pan and keep warm.

4. Heat the remaining oil in the frying pan, add the onion and cook over a low heat, stirring occasionally, for 10–12 minutes, until softened. Gently stir in the rice and cook, stirring, for 1 minute. Pour in the wine and cook, stirring, until it has all been absorbed. Add the reserved mushroom-soaking liquid and cook, stirring, until it has all been absorbed.

5. Gradually add the hot stock, a ladleful at a time. Stir constantly and add more liquid as the rice absorbs each addition. Cook for 20 minutes, or until all the liquid has been absorbed and the rice is creamy but still firm to the bite.

6. Remove from the heat and gently stir in the mushroom mixture, butter and half the Parmesan cheese. Season to taste with salt and pepper.

7. Serve immediately on warmed plates, scattered with the parsley and the remaining cheese.

Sage and Gorgonzola Risotto

SERVES 4

1 litre/1¾ pints hot chicken or vegetable stock

50 g/1¾ oz unsalted butter

150 g/5½ oz pancetta, cubed

1 small onion, chopped

2 garlic cloves, crushed

275 g/9¾ oz risotto rice

125 ml/4 fl oz white wine or vermouth

200 g/7 oz Gorgonzola cheese, crumbled

2 tbsp chopped fresh sage, plus extra leaves to garnish

2 tbsp finely grated Parmesan cheese

salt and pepper

1. Bring the stock to the boil in a saucepan, then reduce the heat and keep simmering gently over a low heat while you are cooking the risotto.

2. Heat half the butter in a large saucepan and cook the pancetta over a medium–high heat, stirring frequently, until the pancetta is beginning to brown. Add the onion and garlic and cook, stirring frequently, for 5 minutes, or until the onion has softened.

3. Add the rice and stir to coat in the pancetta mixture. Pour in the wine and cook, stirring constantly, until almost all the liquid has been absorbed.

4. Gradually add the hot stock, a ladleful at a time. Stir constantly and add more liquid as the rice absorbs each addition. Cook for 20 minutes, or until all the liquid has been absorbed and the rice is creamy but still firm to the bite.

5. Remove from the heat, then add the Gorgonzola cheese and chopped sage and stir until the cheese has melted. Season to taste with salt and pepper, then add the remaining butter and the Parmesan cheese. Garnish with sage leaves and serve immediately

Chicken Risotto with Saffron

SERVES 6–8

1.3 litres/2¼ pints chicken stock

125 g/4½ oz butter

900 g/2 lb skinless, boneless chicken breasts,
    thinly sliced

1 large onion, chopped

500 g/1 lb 2 oz risotto rice

150 ml/5 fl oz white wine

1 tsp crumbled saffron threads

55 g/2 oz grated Parmesan cheese

salt and pepper

1. Bring the stock to the boil in a saucepan, then reduce the heat and keep simmering gently over a low heat while you are cooking the risotto.

2. Meanwhile, heat 4 tablespoons of the butter in a deep saucepan, then add the chicken and onion and cook, stirring frequently, for 8 minutes, or until golden brown.

3. Add the rice and mix to coat in the butter. Cook, stirring constantly, for 2–3 minutes, or until the grains are translucent. Add the wine and cook, stirring constantly, for 1 minute, until reduced.

4. Mix the saffron with 4 tablespoons of the hot stock. Add the liquid to the rice and cook, stirring constantly, until it has been absorbed.

5. Gradually add the remaining hot stock, a ladleful at a time. Stir constantly and add more liquid as the rice absorbs each addition. Cook for 20 minutes, or until all the liquid has been absorbed and the rice is creamy but still firm to the bite. Season to taste with salt and pepper.

6. Remove the risotto from the heat and add the remaining butter. Mix well, then stir in the Parmesan cheese until it melts. Spoon the risotto onto warmed plates and serve immediately.

Venetian Seafood Risotto

SERVES 4

225 g/8 oz large prawns
225 g/8 oz mussels, scrubbed and debearded
225 g/8 oz clams, scrubbed
2 garlic cloves, halved
1 lemon, sliced
600 ml/1 pint water
115 g/4 oz butter
1 tbsp olive oil

1 onion, finely chopped
2 tbsp chopped fresh flat-leaf parsley
350 g/12 oz risotto rice
125 ml/4 fl oz dry white wine
225 g /8 oz cleaned squid, cut into small pieces or rings
4 tbsp Marsala
salt and pepper

1. Peel the prawns, reserving the heads and shells. Cut a slit along the back of each and remove and discard the dark vein. Wrap the heads and shells in a square of muslin and pound with the side of a rolling pin, reserving any liquid they yield. Discard any mussels and clams with broken shells and any that refuse to close when tapped.

2. Place the garlic, lemon, mussels and clams in a saucepan and add the wrapped shells and any reserved liquid. Pour in the water, cover tightly and bring to the boil over a high heat. Cook, shaking the saucepan frequently, for 5 minutes, until the shellfish have opened. Discard any that remain closed. Remove the clams and mussels from their shells and set aside. Strain the cooking liquid. Make up the amount of liquid to 1.2 litres/2 pints with water. Pour this liquid into a saucepan. Bring to the boil, then reduce the heat and keep simmering gently over a low heat while you make the risotto.

3. Melt 25 g/1 oz of the butter with the olive oil in a deep saucepan. Add the onion and half the parsley and cook over a medium heat, stirring occasionally, for 5 minutes, or until softened. Reduce the heat, add the rice and mix to coat in oil and butter. Cook, stirring constantly, for 2–3 minutes, or until the grains are translucent.

4. Add the wine and cook, stirring constantly, for 1 minute, until reduced. Gradually add the hot stock, a ladleful at a time. Stir constantly and add more liquid as the rice absorbs each addition. Cook for 20 minutes, or until all the liquid has been absorbed and the rice is creamy but still firm to the bite.

5. About 5 minutes before the rice is ready, melt 55 g/2 oz of the remaining butter in a heavy-based saucepan. Add the squid and cook, stirring frequently, for 3 minutes, then add the reserved prawns and cook for a further 2–3 minutes, until the squid is opaque and the prawns have changed colour. Stir in the Marsala, bring to the boil and cook until all the liquid has evaporated. Stir the squid, prawns, mussels and clams into the rice, add the remaining butter and parsley and season to taste with salt and pepper. Heat through briefly and serve immediately.

Second Course

The second course (*secondo piatto*) demonstrates the typical Italian inventiveness with a wide range of meat and fish. As well as the classic steaks and roasts, you'll find interesting braises such as Osso Bucco with Orange and Lemon. Literally meaning 'bone hole', this is made with veal marrowbones sliced in hefty chunks and traditionally topped with a lemon rind and parsley garnish known as gremolata. Rosemary-scented pork, roasted until the skin is delectably crisp, is the traditional dish of Umbria. Lamb is often served for special occasions, cooked on a spit or roasted in the oven with wine, garlic and herbs. Very small cutlets from young lambs are a popular delicacy, especially in Rome.

Poultry dishes provide some of Italy's finest food. Every part of the bird is used, including the feet, wings and innards for making soup.

Chicken alla Cacciatore is a classic braise of chicken, white wine and tomatoes. Pan-fried chicken breasts are served everywhere, as is spit-roasted chicken strongly flavoured with rosemary.

Italy has over 7,000 km/4,350 miles of coastline and numerous inland waterways and lakes, so it is hardly surprising that fish and seafood feature highly on the Italian menu. Italians eat everything that comes out of the sea, from the smallest baby fish to the massive tuna. Livorno Seafood Stew typically showcases the wonderful variety of fish and seafood available. In the mountains of the north, river trout are popular, while in the south tuna and swordfish are more likely to be served. Simple techniques such as grilling and searing enhance the fresh natural flavours.

Saltimbocca alla Romana

SERVES 4

8 small, thin veal cutlets, about
    75 g/2¾ oz each
8 slices Parma ham
16 sage leaves

plain flour, for coating
50 g/1¾ oz butter
200 ml/7 fl oz dry white wine
salt and pepper

1. Place the veal cutlets between 2 sheets of clingfilm and carefully pound to an even thickness using a meat mallet or rolling pin. Place a slice of Parma ham and 2 sage leaves on top of each cutlet, then fold in half and secure with a cocktail stick. Spread out the flour on a plate and use to coat the cutlets, tapping off any excess.

2. Melt the butter in a large frying pan and cook the cutlets over a high heat for 2 minutes on each side. Season to taste with salt and pepper, then sprinkle over 2–3 tablespoons of the wine. Once the wine has evaporated, remove the cutlets from the pan and place on a warmed plate.

3. Pour the remaining wine into the frying pan and simmer for 1–2 minutes, scraping any sediment from the base of the pan. Pass through a fine-meshed sieve and pour over the cutlets. Serve immediately.

Osso Bucco with Orange and Lemon

SERVES 6

1–2 tbsp plain flour

6 meaty slices osso bucco (veal shins)

1 kg/2 lb 4 oz fresh tomatoes, peeled, deseeded and diced, or 800 g/1 lb 12 oz canned chopped tomatoes

1–2 tbsp olive oil

2 onions, very finely chopped

2 carrots, finely diced

225 ml/8 fl oz dry white wine

225 ml/8 fl oz veal stock

6 large basil leaves, torn

1 large garlic clove, very finely chopped

finely grated rind of 1 large lemon

finely grated rind of 1 orange

2 tbsp finely chopped fresh flat-leaf parsley

salt and pepper

crusty bread, to serve

1. Place the flour in a polythene bag and season well with salt and pepper. Add the osso bucco, a couple of pieces at a time, and shake until well coated. Remove and shake off the excess flour. Continue until all the pieces are coated. If using canned tomatoes, place in a sieve and leave to drain.

2. Heat 1 tablespoon of the oil in a large, flameproof casserole. Add the osso bucco and fry for 10 minutes on each side until well browned. Remove from the casserole.

3. Add 1–2 teaspoons of oil to the casserole, if necessary. Add the onions and fry for 5 minutes, stirring, until softened. Stir in the carrots and continue frying until softened.

4. Add the tomatoes, wine, stock and basil and return the osso bucco to the casserole. Bring to the boil, then reduce the heat, cover and simmer for 1 hour. Check that the meat is tender with the tip of a knife. If not, continue cooking for 10 minutes and test again.

5. When the meat is tender, sprinkle with the garlic and the lemon and orange rinds, re-cover and cook for a further 10 minutes.

6. Adjust the seasoning, adding salt and pepper if necessary. Sprinkle with the parsley and serve with crusty bread.

Veal with Tuna Sauce

SERVES 4

750 g/1 lb 10 oz loin of veal, boned

2 carrots, thinly sliced

1 onion, thinly sliced

2 celery sticks, thinly sliced

2 cloves

2 bay leaves

1 litre/1¾ pints dry white wine

140 g/5 oz canned tuna, drained

4 anchovy fillets, drained and finely chopped

55 g/2 oz capers, rinsed and finely chopped

55 g/2 oz gherkins, drained and finely chopped

2 egg yolks

4 tbsp lemon juice

125 ml/4 fl oz extra virgin olive oil

salt and pepper

lemon wedges and chopped fresh flat-leaf
   parsley, to garnish

1. Place the veal in a large, non-metallic dish and add the carrots, onion, celery, cloves and bay
    leaves. Pour in the wine and turn the veal to coat. Cover with clingfilm and leave to marinate in the
    refrigerator overnight.

2. Drain the veal, reserving the marinade, and roll up the meat. Wrap it in a piece of muslin, tying it
    with string so that it holds its shape, then place the veal in a large saucepan. Pour the marinade into
    another saucepan and bring to the boil. Pour it over the veal and add sufficient boiling water to
    cover. Season to taste with salt and pepper, bring back to the boil, then lower the heat, cover and
    simmer for 1½ hours, until tender but still firm.

3. Transfer the veal to a plate and set aside to cool completely, then chill until ready to serve. Strain
    the cooking liquid into a bowl and set aside to cool.

4. Combine the tuna, anchovies, capers and gherkins in a bowl or process in a food processor or
    blender to make a purée. Beat the egg yolks with the lemon juice in another bowl. Gradually beat
    in the oil, adding it drop by drop to begin with and then in a steady stream. When all the oil has
    been incorporated, stir in the tuna mixture and about 2 tablespoons of the cooled cooking liquid
    to give the consistency of double cream. Season to taste with salt and pepper. Cover with clingfilm
    and leave to chill in the refrigerator until required.

5. To serve, unwrap the veal and pat it dry with kitchen paper. Using a sharp knife, cut the meat into
    3–10-mm/⅛–¼-inch thick slices and arrange them on a serving platter. Stir the tuna sauce and
    spoon it over the veal. Garnish with the lemon wedges and parsley and serve.

Beef Braised in Red Wine

SERVES 6

3 tbsp olive oil

2 onions, finely sliced

2 garlic cloves, chopped

1 kg/2 lb 4 oz braising beef, cut into thick strips

2 tbsp plain flour

300 ml/10 fl oz good-quality red wine, such as Chianti

2 fresh sage sprigs

200 ml/7 fl oz beef or vegetable stock

1 tbsp tomato purée

salt and pepper

1 tbsp finely chopped fresh flat-leaf parsley, to garnish

1. Preheat the oven to 150°C/300°F/Gas Mark 2. Heat 1 tablespoon of the oil in a large frying pan, add the onions and garlic and cook over a medium heat, stirring frequently, for 6–8 minutes, until softened and browned. Remove with a slotted spoon and transfer to a casserole.

2. Heat the remaining oil in the frying pan, add the beef and cook over a high heat, stirring, for 3–4 minutes, until browned all over. Sprinkle in the flour and stir well to prevent lumps. Season well with salt and pepper. Reduce the heat to medium, pour in the wine, stirring constantly, and bring to the boil, continuing to stir constantly.

3. Carefully turn the contents of the frying pan into the casserole. Add the sage, stock and tomato purée, cover and cook in the centre of the preheated oven for 2½–3 hours.

4. Remove from the oven and discard the sage. Taste and adjust the seasoning, adding salt and pepper if necessary. Serve immediately, scattered with the parsley.

Grilled Steak with Pizzaiola Sauce

SERVES 4

3 tbsp olive oil, plus extra for brushing

700 g/1 lb 9 oz tomatoes, peeled and chopped

1 red pepper, deseeded and chopped

1 onion, chopped

2 garlic cloves, finely chopped

1 tbsp chopped fresh flat-leaf parsley

1 tsp dried oregano

1 tsp sugar

4 x 175 g/6 oz entrecôte or rump steaks

salt and pepper

1. Place the oil, tomatoes, pepper, onion, garlic, parsley, oregano and sugar in a heavy-based saucepan and season to taste with salt and pepper. Bring to the boil, lower the heat and simmer for 15 minutes.

2. Meanwhile, snip any fat around the outsides of the steaks. Season each generously with pepper (no salt) and brush with oil. Preheat the grill to high. Cook the steaks under the preheated grill for 1 minute on each side. Lower the heat to medium and cook according to taste: 1½–2 minutes each side for rare; 2½–3 minutes each side for medium; 3–4 minutes each side for well done.

3. Transfer the steaks to warmed individual plates and spoon over the sauce. Serve immediately.

Roast Pork Loin

SERVES 6

1.8 kg/4 lb flat piece pork loin, chined
  (backbone removed) and rind scored
3 garlic cloves, crushed
2 tbsp chopped fresh rosemary

4 fresh rosemary sprigs, plus extra to garnish
225 ml/8 fl oz dry white wine
salt and pepper

1. Preheat the oven to 230°C/450°F/Gas Mark 8. Put the pork loin on a work surface, skin side
   down. Make small slits in the meat all over the surface. Season very well with salt and pepper. Rub
   the garlic all over the meat surface and sprinkle with the chopped rosemary.

2. Roll up the loin and secure the rosemary sprigs on the outside with fine string. Make sure that the
   joint is securely tied. Season the rind with plenty of salt to give a good crackling.

3. Transfer the meat to a roasting tin and roast in the preheated oven for 20 minutes, or until the fat
   has started to run. Reduce the oven temperature to 190°C/375°F/Gas Mark 5 and pour half the wine
   over the meat. Roast for a further 1 hour 40 minutes, basting occasionally with the pan juices.

4. Remove the meat from the oven and leave to rest in a warm place for 15 minutes before carving.
   Remove the string and rosemary sprigs before cutting into thick slices.

5. Pour off all but 1 tablespoon of the fat from the roasting tin. Add the remaining wine to the juices
   in the tin and bring to the boil, scraping up and stirring in any sediment from the base of the tin.
   Spoon over the meat and serve immediately, garnished with extra sprigs of rosemary.

Sausages with Borlotti Beans

SERVES 4

2 tbsp virgin olive oil

500 g/1 lb 2 oz luganega or other Italian sausage

140 g/5 oz smoked pancetta or streaky bacon, diced

2 red onions, chopped

2 garlic cloves, finely chopped

225 g/8 oz dried borlotti beans, covered and soaked overnight in cold water

2 tsp finely chopped fresh rosemary

2 tsp chopped fresh sage

300 ml/10 fl oz dry white wine

salt and pepper

fresh rosemary sprigs, to garnish

crusty bread, to serve

1. Preheat the oven to 140°C/275°F/Gas Mark 1. Heat the oil in a flameproof casserole. Add the sausages and cook over a low heat, turning frequently, for about 10 minutes, until browned all over. Remove from the casserole and set aside.

2. Add the pancetta to the casserole, increase the heat to medium, and cook, stirring frequently, for 5 minutes, or until golden brown. Remove with a slotted spoon and set aside.

3. Add the onions to the casserole and cook over a low heat, stirring occasionally, for 5 minutes, until softened. Add the garlic and cook for a further 2 minutes.

4. Drain the beans and reserve the soaking liquid. Add the beans to the casserole, then return the sausages and pancetta. Gently stir in the herbs and pour in the wine. Measure the reserved soaking liquid and add 300 ml/10 fl oz to the casserole. Season to taste with salt and pepper. Bring to the boil over a low heat and boil for 15 minutes, then transfer to the preheated oven and cook for 2¾ hours.

5. Remove the casserole from the oven and ladle the sausages and beans onto 4 warmed serving plates. Garnish with the rosemary sprigs and serve immediately with crusty bread.

Grilled Leg of Lamb

SERVES 6–8

1 leg of lamb, about 5 lb/2.25 kg, butterflied
4 garlic cloves, crushed
2 tbsp finely chopped fresh rosemary
finely grated rind and juice of 2 lemons

3 tbsp olive oil
salt and pepper
green salad, to serve

1. Trim any excess fat from the lamb and make small, deep slits in the meat all over the surface. Transfer to a shallow dish and rub all over with the garlic, rosemary and lemon rind. Pour over the oil and lemon juice and season well with salt and pepper. Cover and leave to marinate in the refrigerator, or preferably in a larder or other cool place, for at least 4 hours, or overnight if possible, turning the meat occasionally.

2. Preheat the grill or light a charcoal barbecue and leave to burn until the coals are grey and very hot. Remove the meat from the marinade and pat dry with kitchen paper. Season again with salt and pepper and put on the grill rack. Cook for 2 minutes on both sides until sealed, then reduce the heat to medium–high or lift away from the coals and cook for a further 8 minutes on both sides. Test to see if it is cooked to your taste – it should be charred on the outside but still rare in the centre.

3. Remove from the heat, cover with foil and leave to rest for 15 minutes before carving into long strips. Serve with a green salad.

Chicken alla Cacciatora

SERVES 4

1 small chicken, about 1.3 kg/3 lb
2 tbsp olive oil
50 g/1¾ oz pancetta, diced
1 onion, finely chopped
125 ml/4 fl oz white wine

4 ripe tomatoes
250 ml/9 fl oz chicken stock
salt and pepper
chopped fresh flat-leaf parsley, to garnish

1. Rinse the chicken under cold running water, pat dry with kitchen paper and cut into 8 pieces. Rub the skin with plenty of salt and pepper.

2. Heat the oil in a flameproof casserole and cook the pancetta and onion for 3–4 minutes, until the onion is softened and translucent. Add the chicken pieces and fry on all sides, until golden brown. Stir in the wine, bring to the boil and simmer for 5 minutes.

3. Meanwhile, skin and deseed the tomatoes, then dice the flesh. Add to the casserole with the stock, cover and simmer for 30–40 minutes. Season to taste with salt and pepper and sprinkle with parsley before serving.

Stuffed Chicken Breasts

SERVES 4

4 skinless, boneless chicken breasts, about
150 g/5½ oz each

4 thin slices Italian dry-cured ham

4 slices pecorino cheese

4 cooked asparagus spears, plus extra to serve

1 tbsp plain flour

40 g/1½ oz butter

2 tbsp olive oil

150 ml/5 fl oz dry white wine

50 ml/2 fl oz chicken stock

salt and pepper

1. Put each chicken breast between 2 pieces of clingfilm or inside a polythene food bag and, using a rolling pin, gently beat out until 1 cm/½ inch thick.

2. Season well with salt and pepper and put a slice of ham on top of each chicken breast. Top each with a slice of cheese and an asparagus spear. Roll the breasts up carefully and secure with fine string. Dust with flour and season well with salt and pepper.

3. Heat 30 g/1 oz of the butter with the oil in a large frying pan. Add the chicken rolls and cook over a moderate heat, turning frequently, for 15 minutes, or until cooked through, tender and golden brown. Remove the string, transfer the chicken rolls to a warmed serving dish and keep warm.

4. Add the wine and stock to the frying pan and bring to the boil, scraping up and stirring in any sediment from the base of the frying pan. Bring to the boil and add the remaining butter. Stir well and leave to bubble until thick.

5. Spoon the sauce over the chicken and serve immediately with asparagus spears.

Tuna with Salsa Verde

SERVES 4

4 fresh tuna steaks, about
  2 cm/¾ inch thick
olive oil, for brushing
salt and pepper
lemon wedges, to serve

SALSA VERDE
55 g/2 oz fresh flat-leaf parsley, leaves and
  stems
4 spring onions, chopped
2 garlic cloves, chopped
3 anchovy fillets in oil, drained
30 g/1 oz fresh basil leaves
½ tbsp capers in brine, rinsed and dried
2 sprigs of fresh oregano or ½ tsp dried
  oregano
125 ml/4 fl oz extra virgin olive oil
1–2 tbsp lemon juice, to taste

1. To make the salsa verde, put the parsley, spring onions, garlic, anchovy fillets, basil, capers and oregano in a food processor. Pulse to chop and blend together. With the motor still running, pour in the oil through the feed tube. Add lemon juice to taste, then process again. If it is too thick, add a little extra oil. Cover and chill until required.

2. Place a cast-iron griddle pan over a high heat until you can feel the heat rising from the surface. Brush the tuna steaks with oil and place, oiled side down, on the hot pan and cook for 2 minutes.

3. Lightly brush the top side of the tuna steaks with a little more oil. Use a pair of tongs to turn over the tuna steaks, then season to taste with salt and pepper. Continue cooking for a further 2 minutes for rare or for up to 4 minutes for well done.

4. Transfer the tuna steaks to serving plates and serve with the salsa verde spooned over, accompanied by the lemon wedges.

Trout Fillets with Porcini

SERVES 4

8 wild trout fillets, about 100 g/3½ oz each

1 tbsp chopped fresh tarragon

500 ml/18 fl oz white wine

500 g/1 lb 2 oz fresh porcini or ceps

100 g/3½ oz butter

1 small onion, finely chopped

1 tbsp chopped fresh thyme

salt and pepper

1. Rinse the trout fillets, pat dry with kitchen paper and rub well with salt and pepper. Place in a bowl with the tarragon and 125 ml/4 fl oz of the wine, then cover and leave to marinate for 30 minutes.

2. Wipe the porcini with damp kitchen paper and slice into 1 cm/½ inch thick slices. Melt 50 g/1¾ oz of the butter in a frying pan and cook the onion for 3–4 minutes, until softened and translucent. Add the porcini and cook, stirring, until the juices have evaporated. Stir in the remaining wine with the thyme, season to taste with salt and pepper and cook over a low heat for 10 minutes.

3. Meanwhile, melt the remaining butter in a large, non-stick frying pan over a medium–high heat. Lift the trout fillets out of the marinade, reserving the marinade, and pat dry with kitchen paper. Place the trout in the pan and cook for 3 minutes on each side. Add the reserved marinade to the pan and bring to the boil.

4. Transfer the trout fillets and any juices to serving plates and spoon over the porcini mixture. Serve immediately.

Sole with Artichokes

SERVES 4

8 small purple artichokes
juice of 1 lemon
125 ml/4 fl oz olive oil
4 garlic cloves, thinly sliced
250 ml/9 fl oz dry white wine

400 ml/14 fl oz fish stock
plain flour, for coating
800 g/1 lb 12 oz sole fillets
1 tbsp finely chopped fresh flat-leaf parsley
salt and pepper

1. Clean the artichokes under cold running water. Trim the stems 4 cm/1½ inches from the bottom, remove the hard outer leaves and chop off the sharp tips of the remaining leaves. Cut the artichokes lengthways into strips and immediately place into a bowl of water with the lemon juice. Leave to stand until ready to cook, then drain and pat dry with kitchen paper.

2. Heat 6 tablespoons of the oil in a large pan and sauté the artichokes for 5 minutes. Add the garlic and cook until golden brown. Pour in the wine and stock, season to taste with salt and pepper and simmer gently for 20–25 minutes.

3. Spread out the flour on a plate, season to taste with salt and pepper and use to coat the fish fillets, tapping off any excess. Heat the remaining oil in a large frying pan and cook the fish on both sides, until golden and cooked through.

4. Transfer the artichoke mixture to serving plates and top with the fish. Scatter over the parsley and serve immediately.

Livorno Seafood Stew

SERVES 6

4 red mullet fillets

450 g/1 lb monkfish tail

400 g/14 oz cleaned baby squid

3 tbsp olive oil

1 onion, finely chopped

2 garlic cloves, finely chopped

2 fennel bulbs, finely sliced

150 ml/5 fl oz dry white wine

600 g/1 lb 5 oz canned chopped tomatoes

500 g/1 lb 2 oz live mussels, scrubbed and debearded

750 ml/1¼ pints fish stock

18 large prawns, peeled and deveined

salt and pepper

2 tbsp finely chopped fresh flat-leaf parsley, to garnish

6 slices ciabatta, toasted, rubbed with garlic and drizzled with olive oil, to serve

1. Cut the red mullet fillets into thirds. Cut the monkfish into similar-sized pieces, cutting the flesh away from the tailbone. Cut the squid into thick rings and retain the tentacles.

2. Heat the oil in a large saucepan, add the onion, garlic and fennel and cook over a medium heat, stirring frequently, for 4–5 minutes, until starting to soften. Pour in the wine, stir well and leave to simmer until almost evaporated. Add the tomatoes and bring to the boil, then reduce the heat and simmer, uncovered, for a further 10–15 minutes until the fennel is tender and the sauce is reduced and thickened.

3. Bring the stock to the boil in a separate large saucepan, add the mussels and cook, covered, over a high heat for 3–4 minutes, shaking the saucepan occasionally, until the mussels have opened. Discard any mussels that remain closed. Drain the mussels, reserving the stock. Remove half the mussels from their shells, discarding the shells. Keep all the mussels warm.

4. Add the reserved stock to the tomato mixture and bring to the boil. Add the mullet, monkfish, squid and prawns to the saucepan and cook for 2–3 minutes, until tender and the prawns have turned pink. Add all the mussels and heat through. Season to taste with salt and pepper.

5. Transfer the stew to individual warmed soup dishes, making sure that the seafood is evenly divided. Sprinkle with the chopped parsley and serve with toasted ciabatta slices.

Stuffed Squid

SERVES 4

4 prepared squid, with tentacles

2 shallots

1 garlic clove

100 g/3½ oz cooked ham

3 tbsp cooked rice

1 egg

1 tbsp finely chopped fresh parsley, plus extra
   to garnish

1 tsp grated lemon rind

500 g/1 lb 2 oz fresh tomatoes

1 tbsp olive oil

200 ml/7 fl oz white wine

salt and pepper

1. Wash the squid and pat dry with kitchen paper. Chop the tentacles into small pieces.

2. Finely chop the shallots and garlic, then place in a bowl with the chopped tentacles, ham, rice, egg, parsley and lemon rind and mix well. Season to taste with salt and pepper. Spoon the mixture into the squid tubes and secure each opening with a cocktail stick.

3. Skin and deseed the tomatoes, then finely dice the flesh. Set aside. Heat the oil in a deep frying pan and cook the stuffed squid on all sides. Add the tomatoes and wine and bring to the boil. Reduce the heat, cover and simmer for about 45 minutes. Season to taste with salt and pepper. Transfer the squid to serving plates and spoon over the cooking juices. Garnish with parsley and serve immediately.

Vegetables and Salads

In Italy, vegetables and salads are often eaten on their own, either as antipasti or after the main course in order to better appreciate their bright fresh flavours, textures and colours. This is particularly true of salads, but starchy vegetables such as beans and potatoes are served with the main course since they complement rather than compete with the flavour of meat and fish.

Vegetables grow in abundance in Italy and the Italians have put their heart into using them in the most imaginative and tasty ways. Each region has its specialities: in the south aubergines are a key ingredient in Caponata, a richly flavoured sweet-sour vegetable medley; while asparagus and chicory are popular in the north-east and are typically served grilled or baked in a gratin. Some vegetables are eaten raw;

others are grilled or fried then usually cooled and served with a drizzle of olive oil or fresh lemon juice. A surprising number of vegetables are roasted: not just familiar roots but also fennel and green vegetables, such as broccoli spears or romanesco cauliflower – roasting really intensifies their inherently rich flavours.

The choice of salads is enormous, ranging from a simple dish of mixed leaves or rocket topped with a few shavings of Parmesan, to the robust Panzanella, a Tuscan bread and tomato salad flavoured with basil, vinegar and olive oil. Also popular are heartier dishes of cooked beans dressed in fruity olive oil and herbs. Vegetable salads are always served slightly warm or at room temperature instead of being chilled, which dulls the delicious flavours.

Baked Aubergines with Mozzarella and Parmesan

SERVES 4

4 aubergines, trimmed

3 tbsp olive oil, plus extra for oiling

300 g/10½ oz mozzarella cheese, thinly sliced

4 slices Parma ham, shredded

1 tbsp chopped fresh marjoram

25 g/1 oz Parmesan cheese, grated

salt and pepper

TOMATO SAUCE

4 tbsp olive oil

1 large onion, sliced

4 garlic cloves, crushed

400 g/14 oz canned chopped tomatoes

450 g/1 lb fresh tomatoes, peeled and
   chopped

4 tbsp chopped fresh flat-leaf parsley

600 ml/1 pint hot vegetable stock

1 tbsp sugar

2 tbsp lemon juice

150 ml/5 fl oz dry white wine

salt and pepper

BÉCHAMEL SAUCE

25 g/1 oz butter

25 g/1 oz plain flour

1 tsp mustard powder

300 ml/10 fl oz milk

freshly grated nutmeg

salt and pepper

1. Preheat the oven to 190°C/375°F/Gas Mark 5. Oil a large baking dish.

2. To make the tomato sauce, heat the oil in a large frying pan. Add the onion and garlic and fry until just beginning to soften. Add the canned and fresh tomatoes, parsley, stock, sugar and lemon juice. Cover and simmer for 15 minutes. Stir in the wine and season to taste with salt and pepper.

3. Thinly slice the aubergines lengthways. Bring a large saucepan of water to the boil and cook the aubergine slices for 5 minutes. Drain on kitchen paper and pat dry.

4. Pour half of the fresh tomato sauce into the prepared baking dish. Cover with half of the cooked aubergines and drizzle with a little oil. Cover with half of the mozzarella, Parma ham and marjoram. Season to taste with salt and pepper. Repeat the layers.

5. To make the béchamel sauce, heat the butter in a large saucepan. When it has melted, add the flour and mustard powder. Stir until smooth and cook over a low heat for 2 minutes. Slowly beat in the milk. Simmer gently for 2 minutes. Remove from the heat and season with a large pinch of nutmeg, and salt and pepper to taste.

6. Spoon the béchamel sauce over the aubergine and tomato mixture, then sprinkle with Parmesan cheese. Bake in the preheated oven for 35–40 minutes, until golden on top. Serve immediately.

Caponata

SERVES 4

4 tbsp olive oil
2 celery sticks, sliced
2 red onions, sliced
450 g/1 lb aubergines, diced
1 garlic clove, finely chopped
5 plum tomatoes, chopped
3 tbsp red wine vinegar

1 tbsp sugar
3 tbsp green olives, stoned
2 tbsp capers
salt and pepper
4 tbsp chopped fresh flat-leaf parsley,
   to garnish

1. Heat half the oil in a large, heavy-based saucepan. Add the celery and onions and cook over a low heat, stirring occasionally, for 5 minutes, until softened but not coloured. Add the remaining oil and the aubergines. Cook, stirring frequently, for about 5 minutes, until the aubergines begin to colour.

2. Add the garlic, tomatoes, vinegar and sugar and mix well. Cover the mixture with a circle of greaseproof paper and simmer gently for about 10 minutes.

3. Remove the greaseproof paper, stir in the olives and capers and season to taste with salt and pepper. Tip the caponata into a serving dish and set aside to cool to room temperature.

4. Sprinkle the parsley over the vegetables and serve immediately.

Fennel Gratin

SERVES 4

4 fennel bulbs

1 tbsp lemon juice

25 g/1 oz butter, plus extra for greasing

2 tbsp plain flour

500 ml/18 fl oz lukewarm milk

100 ml/3½ fl oz double cream

2 tbsp white wine

½ tsp freshly grated nutmeg

125 g/4½ oz fontina cheese, grated

50 g/1¾ oz pine kernels

salt and pepper

1. Preheat the oven to 180°C/350°F/Gas Mark 4. Grease a large baking dish.

2. Trim the fennel, reserving the green leaves. Cut the fennel bulbs into 5 mm/¼ thick slices. Bring a large saucepan of lightly salted water to the boil. Add the fennel and lemon juice, bring back to the boil and blanch for 3 minutes. Using a slotted spoon, lift out the fennel and transfer to a bowl of iced water to stop the cooking. When cool, transfer to a colander and drain well.

3. Melt the butter in a saucepan, add the flour and cook over a low heat, stirring, for 1–2 minutes. Gradually add the milk and cream, stirring constantly. Bring to the boil and simmer gently until thickened. Stir in the wine and nutmeg, then season to taste with salt and pepper.

4. Place the fennel in the prepared dish, pour over the sauce and scatter over the fontina cheese. Transfer to the preheated oven and cook for 25 minutes, until golden brown.

5. Meanwhile, toast the pine kernels in a dry frying pan. Chop the reserved fennel leaves. Scatter the pine kernels and fennel leaves over the gratin before serving.

Courgette Flower Fritters

SERVES 4–6

100 g/3½ oz self-raising flour
1 tsp baking powder
1 tbsp extra virgin olive oil
1 egg, beaten
200–250 ml/7–9 fl oz iced water

olive oil, for shallow-frying
16–20 courgette flowers
salt and pepper
sea salt flakes and lemon wedges, to serve

1. Sift the flour and baking powder together into a bowl and add the extra virgin olive oil and egg. Stir in enough of the water to make a batter with the consistency of double cream (the exact quantity may vary according to the flour used). Season to taste with salt and a little pepper.

2. Pour a shallow layer of olive oil into a large frying pan or wok and heat over a high heat until hot. Dip the courgette flowers briefly in the batter, add to the oil and cook, in batches, for 2–4 minutes until crisp and golden. Remove with a slotted spoon and drain on kitchen paper. Serve immediately, lightly sprinkled with sea salt flakes and with lemon wedges for squeezing over.

Spinach in Gorgonzola Sauce

SERVES 4

1 kg/2 lb 4 oz spinach
60 g/2¼ oz butter
½ tsp freshly grated nutmeg
125 ml/4 fl oz white wine

125 ml/4 fl oz milk
125 g/4½ oz Gorgonzola cheese
2 egg yolks
salt and pepper

1. Remove and discard any tough stems from the spinach, then place the leaves in a colander and wash under cold running water. Leave to drain.

2. Melt half the butter in a large saucepan over a medium heat. Stir in the spinach, with the water still clinging to its leaves, cover and cook for 3–4 minutes, until wilted. Stir in the nutmeg and season to taste with salt and pepper, then reduce the heat to low to keep the spinach warm while you prepare the sauce.

3. Pour the wine and milk into a separate pan, bring to the boil, then simmer until reduced slightly. Add the Gorgonzola and stir until melted. Remove from the heat. Beat the egg yolks in a small bowl, stir in a little of the hot sauce, then tip back into the pan with the remaining butter and the spinach. Taste and adjust the seasoning, adding salt and pepper if needed. Serve immediately.

Asparagus Gratin

SERVES 4–6

butter, for greasing
1 kg/2 lb 4 oz asparagus spears
pinch of sugar
100 g/3½ oz fontina cheese, sliced

50 g/1¾ oz Parmesan cheese, grated
100 ml/3½ fl oz double cream
salt and pepper

1. Preheat the oven to 240°C/475°F/Gas Mark 9. Grease a large baking dish.

2. Wash the asparagus, then cut off and discard the woody ends. Bring a large saucepan of lightly salted water to the boil. Add the asparagus and sugar, bring back to the boil and simmer for about 15 minutes, until tender but still firm to the bite. Drain.

3. Transfer the asparagus to the prepared baking dish. Place the fontina cheese on top, sprinkle over the Parmesan and pour over the cream. Bake in the preheated oven for 8 minutes, until the topping is golden brown. Sprinkle with pepper and serve immediately.

Rosemary Potatoes

SERVES 4

3 sprigs fresh rosemary

800 g/1 lb 12 oz small potatoes cubed

3 garlic cloves, roughly chopped

5 tbsp olive oil, plus extra for oiling

salt and pepper

1. Preheat the oven to 200°C/400°F/Gas Mark 6.

2. Brush a large baking dish with oil. Remove the leaves from the rosemary sprigs, discarding the stems, and chop roughly. Set aside.

3. Place a layer of potatoes in the baking dish, then sprinkle over a little of the garlic and rosemary and season to taste with salt and pepper. Repeat the layers until all the potatoes, garlic and rosemary have been used up.

4. Drizzle over the oil, then transfer to the preheated oven and cook, stirring frequently, for 45 minutes, or until the potatoes are tender and lightly browned.

Roasted Vegetable Salad

SERVES 4

1 onion
1 aubergine
1 red pepper, deseeded
1 orange pepper, deseeded
1 large courgette
2–4 garlic cloves

2–4 tbsp olive oil
1 tbsp balsamic vinegar
2 tbsp extra virgin olive oil
salt and pepper
1 tbsp shredded fresh basil, to garnish
Parmesan cheese shavings, to serve

1. Preheat the oven to 200°C/400°F/Gas Mark 6.

2. Cut all the vegetables into even-sized wedges, put into a roasting tin and scatter over the garlic cloves. Pour over 2 tablespoons of the olive oil and toss the vegetables until well coated. Season to taste with salt and pepper. Roast in the preheated oven for 40 minutes, or until tender, adding the extra olive oil if needed.

3. Meanwhile, put the vinegar, extra virgin olive oil and salt and pepper to taste into a screw-top jar and shake until blended.

4. Once the vegetables are cooked, remove from the oven, arrange on a serving dish and pour over the dressing. Sprinkle with the basil and serve with Parmesan cheese shavings.

Panzanella

SERVES 4

8 large ripe tomatoes

2 garlic cloves, crushed

6 tbsp extra virgin olive oil, plus extra to serve

2 tbsp red wine vinegar or balsamic vinegar

225 g/8 oz two-day-old Tuscan saltless bread or
other rustic country bread

1 red onion, halved through the root and cut
into fine crescent shapes

small handful of fresh basil leaves, roughly torn

salt and pepper

1. Halve the tomatoes and remove and discard the seeds, then cut the flesh into eighths. Put in a
sieve over a bowl to collect the juice.

2. Add the garlic to the tomato juice and season well with salt and pepper. Pour in the oil and vinegar
and stir well. Break the bread up into rough pieces and put in a large bowl. Pour over the tomato
juice mixture and gently stir until the bread has absorbed all the juice. Rub the bread between your
fingers to break it into smaller pieces, handling it very carefully to avoid breaking it up too much.

3. Place a layer of the soaked bread in a serving dish and spoon over half the tomatoes and onion.
Add another layer of bread and top with the remaining tomatoes and onion and the basil. Cover
and leave to stand at room temperature for 1 hour for the flavours to be absorbed by the bread.

4. Stir well, taste and adjust the seasoning, adding salt and pepper if necessary, and drizzle with a little
extra oil before serving.

Broad Bean and Pecorino Salad

SERVES 6

225 g/8 oz shelled fresh broad beans

5 tbsp extra virgin olive oil

2 tbsp freshly squeezed lemon juice

1 tbsp chopped fresh mint

175 g/6 oz young unaged pecorino cheese, cut into cubes

90 g/3¼ oz rocket leaves

55 g/2 oz aged pecorino or Parmesan cheese shavings

salt and pepper

1. If the beans are extremely fresh and tiny, you can serve them raw, but otherwise blanch them for 2–3 minutes in a large saucepan of boiling water. Drain, rinse under cold running water and drain again.

2. Put the drained beans in a dish, pour over the oil and lemon juice and add the mint. Season well with salt and pepper and mix in the pecorino cheese cubes.

3. Arrange the rocket leaves on a serving dish and spoon over the bean and cheese mixture. Scatter over the cheese shavings and serve.

Three-colour Salad

SERVES 4

280 g/10 oz buffalo mozzarella, drained and
    thinly sliced
8 beef tomatoes, sliced

20 fresh basil leaves
125 ml/4 fl oz extra virgin olive oil
salt and pepper

1. Arrange the mozzarella and tomato slices on 4 individual serving plates and season to taste with salt. Set aside in a cool place for 30 minutes.

2. Sprinkle the basil leaves over the salad and drizzle with the olive oil. Season with pepper and serve immediately.

Green and White Bean Salad

SERVES 4

100 g/3½ oz haricot beans, soaked overnight
225 g/8 oz fine French beans, trimmed
¼ red onion, thinly sliced
12 pitted black olives
1 tbsp chopped chives
salt

DRESSING
½ tbsp lemon juice
½ tsp Dijon mustard
6 tbsp extra virgin olive oil
salt and pepper

1. Drain the haricot beans and put them into a saucepan with plenty of fresh water to cover. Bring to the boil, then boil rapidly for 15 minutes. Reduce the heat slightly and cook for a further 30 minutes, or until tender but not disintegrating. Add salt in the last 5 minutes of cooking. Drain and set aside.

2. Meanwhile, plunge the French beans into a large pan of boiling water. Bring back to the boil and cook for 4 minutes, until just tender but still brightly coloured. Drain and set aside.

3. Mix together the dressing ingredients, then leave to stand. While both types of bean are still slightly warm, tip them into a shallow serving dish or arrange on individual plates. Scatter over the onion slices, olives and chives. Stir the dressing again and spoon over the salad. Serve immediately, at room temperature.

Beetroot with Balsamic Vinegar

SERVES 4

500 g/1 lb 2 oz beetroot
2 tbsp balsamic vinegar
1 tbsp mustard

5 tbsp olive oil
small bunch of fresh mint
salt and pepper

1. Preheat the oven to 200°C/400°F/Gas Mark 6. Wash the beetroot and pat dry with kitchen paper. Wrap each beetroot individually in aluminium foil, place on a baking tray and cook in the preheated oven for 40–60 minutes, depending on size.

2. Remove and discard the foil and leave the beetroot to cool slightly. When cool enough to handle, peel the beetroot: it is advisable to wear a pair of disposable polythene gloves for this job or the juices will stain your hands. Cut the beetroot into thin slices and transfer to a serving plate.

3. Place the vinegar, mustard and oil in a small bowl, season to taste with salt and pepper and mix well. Pour over the beetroot slices, sprinkle over the mint and serve.

Orange Salad

SERVES 4

4 oranges

1 red onion

2 tbsp finely chopped fresh flat-leaf parsley,
  plus extra to garnish

4 tbsp olive oil

salt and pepper

1. Using a sharp knife, chop the top and bottom off each orange, then remove and discard the peel and white pith. Cut crossways into thin slices and arrange on a large serving plate.

2. Chop the onion in half through the root, then cut one half of the onion into thin slices. Finely chop the remaining onion half and mix together with the parsley. Scatter these ingredients over the orange slices and season with a little salt and pepper. Drizzle over the oil.

3. Cover with plastic wrap and let marinate in the refrigerator for 1 hour. Remove from the refrigerator 5 minutes before serving, garnished with parsley sprigs.

Radicchio Salad

SERVES 4

400 g/14 oz radicchio leaves
1 tbsp olive oil
100 g/3½ oz pancetta, cut into small cubes

2 tbsp balsamic vinegar
salt and pepper

1. Wash the radicchio leaves and shake dry. Tear the leaves into bite-sized pieces, then divide between 4 serving plates.

2. Heat the oil in a frying pan over medium heat and cook the pancetta for 4–5 minutes, until crispy. Pour in the vinegar and season to taste with salt and pepper.

3. Drizzle the pancetta mixture over the radicchio and serve immediately.

Bread, Pizza and Desserts

Good bread is an essential part of the Italian meal – it appears on the table without fail for you to nibble on while waiting for the first course. Types of bread vary from region to region: soft spongy *focaccia*, sometimes flavoured with onion and rosemary, is hugely popular in Liguria, while *grissini* (dry bread sticks) are a speciality of Piemonte. Italians do not butter their bread; instead they use it to scoop up the sauce remaining in the pasta bowl or tasty meat juices from the main course.

Pizza is known the world over but to create the irresistible aroma and taste of an authentic Italian pizza you will need a home-made dough base and a freshly made tomato sauce. A true pizza is crisp and chewy with a soft integral topping that melts into the base. A classic is Pizza

Margherita, with its simple topping of tomatoes, mozzarella and basil, but this recipe can easily be adapted to use your favourite toppings. Other variations include the *bianca* without any tomatoes, and stuffed pizza turnover, or *calzone*.

Desserts in Italy are often simple affairs consisting of a bowl of fresh seasonal fruit, or a freshly made fruit salad. However, there are more sumptuous concoctions. Tiramisu and Panna Cotta are well known, but there is also Zuccotto, a dome-shaped moulded dessert consisting of rum-soaked sponge fingers filled with whipped cream, almonds and chocolate. The Italians also love cakes and pastries, particularly for special celebrations or to enjoy after a family Sunday lunch.

Focaccia with Onion and Rosemary

MAKES 1 LOAF

450 g/1 lb strong white flour,
  plus extra for dusting

1½ tsp easy-blend dried yeast

½ tsp salt

2 tbsp chopped fresh rosemary, plus extra
  sprigs to garnish

5 tbsp extra virgin olive oil, plus extra for oiling

300 ml/10 fl oz warm water

1 red onion, finely sliced and separated into
  rings

1 tbsp coarse sea salt

1. Mix the flour, yeast and salt together in a mixing bowl, then stir in the chopped rosemary. Make a well in the centre. Mix 3 tablespoons of the oil and water together in a jug and pour into the well. Gradually mix the liquid into the flour mixture with a round-bladed knife. Gather the mixture together with your hands to form a soft dough.

2. Turn the dough out onto a lightly floured work surface and knead for 8–10 minutes, until smooth and elastic. Return the dough to the bowl, cover with a clean tea towel or oiled clingfilm and leave to rise in a warm place for ¾ –1 hour, or until doubled in size. Turn out and gently knead again for 1 minute until smooth.

3. Preheat the oven to 200°C/400°F/Gas Mark 6. Oil a baking sheet. Gently roll the dough out to a round about 30 cm/12 inches in diameter – it doesn't have to be a perfect circle; a slightly oval shape is traditional. Transfer to the prepared baking sheet, cover with a clean tea towel or oiled clingfilm and leave to rise in a warm place for 20–30 minutes.

4. Make holes about 5 cm/2 inches apart all over the surface of the dough with the handle of a wooden spoon. Spread the onion rings over the dough, drizzle with the remaining oil and scatter over the salt. Bake in the preheated oven for 20–25 minutes, until well risen and golden brown. Five minutes before the end of the cooking time, garnish with the rosemary sprigs. Transfer to a wire rack to cool for a few minutes, then serve the bread warm.

Ciabatta

MAKES 3 LOAVES

400 ml/14 fl oz lukewarm water
4 tbsp lukewarm semi-skimmed milk
500 g/1 lb 2 oz strong white bread flour
1 sachet easy-blend dried yeast
2 tsp salt
3 tbsp olive oil

BIGA

350 g/12 oz strong white bread flour, plus extra
  for dusting
1¼ tsp easy-blend dried yeast
200 ml/7 fl oz lukewarm water

1. First, make the biga. Sift the flour into a bowl, stir in the yeast and make a well in the centre. Pour in the lukewarm water and stir until the dough comes together. Turn out onto a lightly floured surface and knead for 5 minutes, until smooth and elastic. Shape the dough into a ball, put it in a bowl and put the bowl into a plastic bag or cover with a damp tea towel. Leave to rise in a warm place for 12 hours, until just beginning to collapse.

2. Mix the water and milk into the biga, beating with a wooden spoon. Gradually mix in the flour and yeast with your hand, adding them a little at a time. Finally, mix in the salt and oil. The dough will be very wet, but do not add extra flour. Put the bowl in a plastic bag or cover with a damp tea towel and leave to rise in a warm place for 2 hours, until the dough has doubled in volume.

3. Dust 3 baking sheets with flour. Using a spatula, divide the dough among the prepared baking sheets without knocking out the air. With lightly floured hands, gently pull and shape each piece of dough into a rectangular loaf, then flatten slightly. Dust the tops of the loaves with flour and leave to rise in a warm place for 30 minutes.

4. Meanwhile, preheat the oven to 220°C/425°F/Gas Mark 7. Bake the loaves for 25–30 minutes, until the crust is lightly golden and they sound hollow when tapped on the base with your knuckles. Transfer to wire racks to cool.

Olive Bread

MAKES 3 SMALL LOAVES

500 g/1 lb 2 oz strong white flour, plus extra
   for dusting
1 sachet easy-blend dried yeast
1 tsp salt
pinch of sugar

300 ml/10 fl oz lukewarm water
250 g/9 oz chard, chopped
100 g/3½ oz stoned black olives, chopped
2 tbsp olive oil, plus extra for brushing

1. Sift the flour into a large bowl and make a well in the centre. Pour the yeast, salt and sugar into the well with the water. Gradually incorporate the flour into the liquid, using your fingers, and bring the mixture together to form a dough. Turn out onto a lightly floured counter and knead the dough for 5–10 minutes, until smooth and elastic. Shape the dough into a ball, put it in the bowl and cover with clingfilm. Leave to rise in a warm place for about 1 hour, until the dough has doubled in volume.

2. Brush a baking tray with oil. Knock back the dough with your fist and turn out onto a lightly floured work surface. Knead the chard and olives into the dough and divide into 3 pieces. Form each piece of dough into an oblong loaf and place on the prepared baking tray. Dust a tea towel with flour, place over the baking tray and leave to rise for 1 hour.

3. Preheat the oven to 220°C/425°F/Gas Mark 7. Brush the loaves with oil and bake in the preheated oven for 20–25 minutes. Turn out onto a wire rack and leave to cool.

Pizza Margherita

MAKES 1 PIZZA

PIZZA DOUGH

175 g/6 oz plain flour, plus extra for dusting

1 tsp salt

1 tsp easy-blend dried yeast

1 tbsp olive oil, plus extra for brushing and drizzling

6 tbsp lukewarm water

TOPPING

175 ml/6 fl oz ready-made pizza tomato sauce or 350 g/12 oz tomatoes, peeled and halved

1 garlic clove, thinly sliced

55 g/2 oz mozzarella cheese, thinly sliced

1 tsp dried oregano

fresh basil sprigs, to garnish

salt and pepper

1. Sift the flour and salt together into a bowl and stir in the yeast. Make a well in the centre and pour in the oil and lukewarm water. Stir well with a wooden spoon until the dough begins to come together, then knead with your hands until it leaves the sides of the bowl. Turn out onto a lightly floured surface and knead well for 5–10 minutes, until smooth and elastic.

2. Brush a bowl with oil. Shape the dough into a ball, put it in the bowl and put the bowl into a plastic bag or cover with a damp tea towel. Leave to rise in a warm place for 1 hour, until doubled in volume.

3. Brush a baking sheet with oil. Turn out the dough onto a lightly floured surface, knock back with your fist and knead for 1 minute. Roll or press out the dough to a 25-cm/10-in round. Place on the prepared baking sheet and push up the edge slightly all round. Put the baking sheet in a plastic bag or cover with a damp tea towel and leave to rise in a warm place for 10 minutes.

4. Preheat the oven to 200°C/400°F/Gas Mark 6. Spread the tomato sauce if using, over the pizza base almost to the edge. If using fresh tomatoes, squeeze out some of the juice and coarsely chop the flesh. Spread them evenly over the pizza base and drizzle with olive oil. Sprinkle the garlic over the tomato, add the mozzarella, sprinkle with the oregano and season with salt and pepper. Bake in the preheated oven for 15–20 minutes, until the crust is golden brown and crisp. Brush the crust with oil, garnish with basil and serve immediately.

Calzone

SERVES 4

2 tbsp olive oil, plus extra for brushing
1 red onion, thinly sliced
1 garlic clove, chopped finely
400 g/14 oz canned chopped tomatoes
55 g/2 oz black olives, stoned

2 quantities Pizza Dough (see page 164)
plain flour, for dusting
200 g/7 oz mozzarella cheese, diced
1 tbsp chopped fresh oregano
salt and pepper

1. Preheat the oven to 200°C/400°F/Gas Mark 6. Brush two baking sheets with oil.

2. Heat the oil in a frying pan, add the onion and garlic, and cook over a low heat, stirring occasionally, for 5 minutes, until softened. Add the tomatoes and cook, stirring occasionally, for a further 5 minutes. Stir in the olives and season to taste with salt and pepper. Remove the frying pan from the heat.

3. Divide the pizza dough into 4 pieces. Roll out each piece on a lightly floured surface to form a 20-cm/8-inch round.

4. Divide the tomato mixture between the rounds, spreading it over half of each almost to the edge. Top with the mozzarella cheese and sprinkle with the oregano. Brush the edge of each round with a little water and fold over the uncovered sides. Press the edges to seal.

5. Bake for about 15 minutes, until golden and crisp. Remove from the oven and leave to stand for 2 minutes, then transfer to warmed plates and serve.

Grissini

MAKES 30

350 g/12 oz strong white flour, plus extra
    for dusting
1½ tsp salt
1½ tsp easy-blend dried yeast

200 ml/7 fl oz lukewarm water
3 tbsp olive oil, plus extra for brushing
sesame seeds, for coating

1. Sift the flour and salt together into a warmed bowl. Stir in the yeast and make a well in the centre.
   Add the water and oil to the well and mix to form a soft dough.

2. Turn out the dough onto a lightly floured work surface and knead for 5–10 minutes, or until smooth
   and elastic. Put the dough in an oiled bowl, cover with a damp tea towel and leave to rise in a warm
   place for 1 hour, or until doubled in volume.

3. Preheat the oven to 200°C/400°F/Gas Mark 6. Lightly oil two baking trays.

4. Turn out the dough again and knead lightly. Roll out into a rectangle measuring 23 x 20 cm/
   9 x 8 inches. Cut the dough into 3 strips, each 20 cm/8 inches long, then cut each strip across into
   10 equal pieces.

5. Gently roll and stretch each piece of dough into a stick about 30 cm/12 inches long, then brush
   with oil. Spread out the sesame seeds on a large, shallow plate or tray. Roll each breadstick in the
   sesame seeds to coat, then space well apart on the prepared baking trays. Brush with oil, cover with
   a damp tea towel and leave to prove in a warm place for 15 minutes.

6. Bake the breadsticks in the preheated oven for 10 minutes. Turn over and bake for a further
   5–10 minutes, until golden. Transfer to a wire rack and leave to cool.

Almond Biscotti

MAKES 20–30

250 g/9 oz whole blanched almonds
200 g/7 oz plain flour, plus 1 tbsp for dusting
175 g/6 oz caster sugar, plus 1 tbsp
   for sprinkling

1 tsp baking powder
½ tsp ground cinnamon
2 eggs
2 tsp vanilla extract

1. Preheat the oven to 180°C/350°F/Gas Mark 4. Line 2 baking sheets with baking paper.

2. Very roughly chop the almonds, leaving some whole. Mix the flour, sugar, baking powder and cinnamon together in a mixing bowl. Stir in all the almonds.

3. Beat the eggs with the vanilla extract in a small bowl, then add to the flour mixture and mix together to form a firm dough.

4. Turn the dough out onto a lightly floured work surface and knead lightly. Divide the dough in half and shape each piece into a long, thick log, about 5 cm/2 inches wide. Transfer to the prepared baking sheets, sprinkle with sugar and bake in the preheated oven for 20–25 minutes, until brown and firm.

5. Remove from the oven and leave to cool for a few minutes, then transfer the logs to a chopping board and cut into 1-cm/½-inch slices. Meanwhile, reduce the oven temperature to 160°C/325°F/ Gas Mark 3.

6. Arrange the biscotti slices, cut sides down, on the baking sheets. Bake in the oven for 15–20 minutes, until dry and crisp. Remove from the oven and leave to cool on a wire rack. Store in an airtight container to keep crisp.

Panforte di Siena

SERVES 16

175 g/6 fl oz honey

140 g/5 oz caster sugar

115 g/4 oz candied lemon peel, finely chopped

115 g/4 oz candied orange peel, finely chopped

100 g/3½ oz ground almonds

100 g/3½ oz whole blanched almonds, roughly chopped

100 g/3½ oz whole blanched hazelnuts, roughly chopped

55 g/2 oz plain flour

2 tbsp cocoa powder

1 tsp ground cinnamon

½ tsp ground cloves

a good grating of nutmeg

icing sugar, for dusting

1. Preheat the oven to 160°C/325°F/Gas Mark 3. Oil a 20-cm/8-inch round, shallow cake tin with a removable base.

2. Put the honey and sugar in a small saucepan and heat over a low heat, stirring, until the sugar has dissolved.

3. Put the candied peels in a large mixing bowl and add the nuts. Sift in the flour and cocoa powder and add all the spices. Mix well together. Pour the honey and sugar mixture over the dry ingredients and mix together thoroughly.

4. Turn the mixture into the prepared tin and press down well so that the surface is smooth. Bake in the preheated oven for 30–40 minutes, until firm.

5. Remove from the oven and leave to cool completely in the tin before removing. Dust heavily with icing sugar before serving in slices. The cake will keep in an airtight container or wrapped in clingfilm and aluminium foil for up to 3 months.

Soft Chocolate Cake

SERVES 6–8

280 g/10 oz plain chocolate with at least 72% cocoa solids, broken into pieces

140 g/5 oz unsalted butter, plus extra for greasing

4 eggs, separated

55 g/2 oz caster sugar

25 g/1 oz plain flour

1 tsp vanilla extract

cocoa powder, for dusting

1. Preheat the oven to 180°C/350°F/Gas Mark 4. Grease a 20-cm/8-inch round springform cake tin and line the base with baking paper.

2. Put the chocolate and butter in a heatproof bowl set over a saucepan of gently simmering water and heat until melted. Remove the bowl from the heat and leave to cool for 5 minutes.

3. Beat the eggs yolks and sugar together in a mixing bowl with a handheld electric mixer until thick and creamy. In a separate mixing bowl, beat the egg whites until thick and glossy.

4. Fold the egg yolk mixture into the melted chocolate. Sift in the flour and fold in together with the vanilla extract. Gently fold in the beaten egg whites.

5. Turn the mixture into the prepared tin and bake in the preheated oven for 15–20 minutes. Do not overcook – the top should be firm but the centre still slightly gooey. Remove from the oven, cover, and let cool overnight.

6. Remove the cake tin and peel away the lining paper from the bottom of the cake. Dust the surface of the cake with cocoa powder and serve in slices.

Zuccotto

SERVES 12

2 shop-bought sponge flan cases
3 tbsp lemon liqueur
600 ml/1 pint double cream

150 g/5½ oz icing sugar
100 g/3½ oz plain chocolate, finely grated
150 g/5½ oz almonds, chopped

1. Using a serrated knife, cut the rims off the flan cases to make them an even thickness. Cut 1 flan case into 12 wedges and use to line a large bowl. Sprinkle over 2 tablespoons of the liqueur.

2. In a large bowl, whisk together the cream and 100 g/3½ oz of the icing sugar until stiff. Transfer half the cream mixture to a separate bowl and stir in the chocolate, then spoon into the lined bowl and smooth the surface. Stir the almonds into the remaining cream mixture and spoon on top of the chocolate layer, smoothing the surface. Place the second flan case on top, press down lightly and sprinkle over the remaining liqueur. Transfer to the freezer for at least 6 hours.

3. To serve, turn out onto a serving plate and dust with icing sugar.

Sicilian Cassata

SERVES 12

600 g/1 lb 5 oz ricotta cheese

2 tbsp orange flower water

350 g/12 oz granulated sugar

250 ml/9 fl oz water

300 g/10½ oz crystallized fruit, finely chopped

100 g/3½ oz plain chocolate, finely chopped

50 g/1¾ oz pistachio nuts, chopped

2 shop-bought sponge flan cases

4 tbsp cherry liqueur

2 tbsp lemon juice

1. Mix together the ricotta and orange flower water until smooth. Place 200 g/7 oz of the sugar and the water in a small saucepan and place over a medium heat until the sugar has dissolved. Simmer until reduced slightly, making sure that it does not burn. Remove from the heat and leave to cool slightly. Stir into the ricotta mixture with 150 g/5½ oz of the crystallized fruit, the chocolate and pistachio nuts.

2. Using a serrated knife, cut the rims off the flan cases to make them an even thickness. Cut 1 flan case into 12 wedges and use to line a large pudding basin or bowl. Sprinkle over 2 tablespoons of the liqueur. Spoon the ricotta mixture into the lined pudding basin and smooth the surface. Place the second flan case on top and press down lightly. Transfer to the refrigerator and leave to chill for at least 5 hours, until firm. Turn out onto a serving plate.

3. Place the remaining sugar in a saucepan with the remaining liqueur, the lemon juice and a little water. Heat gently until the sugar has dissolved and the liquid is reduced and syrupy. Pour the syrup over the cassata, then decorate with the remaining crystallized fruit. Chill in the refrigerator for a further hour before serving.

Quick Tiramisu

SERVES 4

225 g/8 oz mascarpone cheese or soft cheese

1 egg, separated

2 tbsp plain yogurt

2 tbsp caster sugar

2 tbsp dark rum

2 tbsp cold strong black coffee

8 sponge fingers

2 tbsp grated plain chocolate

1. Put the mascarpone cheese, egg yolk and yogurt in a large bowl and beat together until smooth.

2. Whip the egg white in a separate, grease-free bowl until stiff but not dry, then beat in the sugar and gently fold into the cheese mixture. Divide half the mixture between 4 sundae glasses.

3. Mix the rum and coffee together in a shallow dish. Dip the sponge fingers into the rum mixture, break them in half, or into smaller pieces if necessary, and divide between the glasses.

4. Stir any remaining coffee mixture into the remaining cheese mixture and divide between the glasses.

5. Sprinkle with the grated chocolate. Serve immediately or cover and chill in the refrigerator until required.

Stuffed Peaches with Amaretto

SERVES 4

55 g/2 oz butter

4 peaches

2 tbsp soft light brown sugar

55 g/2 oz amaretti biscuits or macaroons, crushed

2 tbsp amaretto

125 ml/4 fl oz single cream, to serve

1. Preheat the oven to 180°C/350°F/Gas Mark 4. Use 1 tablespoon of the butter to grease a 20-cm/8-inch gratin dish, or a baking dish large enough to hold 8 peach halves in a single layer.

2. Halve the peaches and remove and discard the stones. If you like, you can skin the peaches: put them in a heatproof bowl of boiling water for 10–15 seconds, then transfer with a slotted spoon to a bowl of cold water and, when cool enough to handle, peel away the skins.

3. Beat the remaining butter and the sugar together in a bowl until creamy, add the biscuit crumbs and mix well.

4. Arrange the peach halves, cut side up, in the prepared baking dish, and fill the stone cavities with the biscuit mixture. Bake in the centre of the preheated oven for 20–25 minutes, or until the peaches are tender. Pour over the amaretto and serve hot with the cream.

Zabaglione

SERVES 4

5 egg yolks
100 g/3½ oz caster sugar

150 ml/5 fl oz Marsala or sweet sherry
amaretti biscuits, to serve

1. Place the egg yolks in a large heatproof bowl. Add the caster sugar to the egg yolks and whisk until the mixture is thick and pale and has doubled in volume.

2. Place the bowl containing the egg yolk and sugar mixture over a saucepan of gently simmering water. Add the Marsala or sherry to the egg yolk and sugar mixture and continue whisking until the foam mixture becomes warm. This process may take as long as 10 minutes.

3. Pour the mixture, which should be frothy and light, into 4 wine glasses. Serve the zabaglione warm with amaretti biscuits.

Panna Cotta

SERVES 6

1 tbsp vegetable oil
1 vanilla pod
600 ml/1 pint double cream
4 tbsp caster sugar

2 tsp powdered gelatine
3 tbsp cold water
6 sprigs fresh mint
about 18 strawberries, sliced

1. Use the oil to grease six 125-ml/4-fl oz ramekins or dariole moulds well.

2. Split the vanilla pod with a sharp knife and scrape out all the seeds. Put the pod and the seeds in a saucepan with the cream and sugar and stir well over a low heat. Carefully bring to simmering point and simmer gently for 2–3 minutes. Remove from the heat and leave to cool a little.

3. Soak the gelatine in 3 tablespoons of cold water in a small heatproof bowl. Place the bowl over a saucepan of hot water and heat gently until the gelatine is dissolved and clear.

4. Remove the vanilla pod from the cream and stir in the gelatine. Pour the mixture into the prepared moulds, cover with clingfilm and chill for at least 3 hours, or overnight, until set.

5. To serve, dip the moulds up to the rim (do not immerse completely) in hot water for 2 seconds and then turn out onto serving plates. Serve decorated with the mint sprigs and fresh berries.

Citrus Granita

SERVES 6

6 oranges
1½ lemons
140 g/5 oz sugar

450 ml/16 fl oz water
6 amaretti biscuits, to serve

1. Pare the rind from the fruit and cut off and discard the pith. Slice a few thin strips of rind and reserve them separately from the large pieces. Squeeze the juice from the fruit.

2. Boil the sugar and water in a heavy-based saucepan and stir until the sugar dissolves. Boil, without stirring, for 10 minutes, until syrupy. Remove from the heat, stir in the large pieces of rind, cover and leave to cool.

3. Strain the cooled syrup into a freezerproof container and stir in the juice. Freeze, uncovered, for 4 hours, until slushy.

4. Blanch the thin rind strips in a saucepan of boiling water for 2 minutes. Drain and refresh with cold water. Pat dry with kitchen paper.

5. Remove the granita from the freezer and break up with a fork. Freeze again for a further 4 hours, or until hard.

6. Remove the granita from the freezer and leave until slightly softened. Beat with a fork, then spoon into glasses and decorate with the rind strips. Serve with biscuits.

Index